The 20 British Prime Ministers
of the 20th century

Churchill

CHRIS WRIGLEY

HAUS PUBLISHING · LONDON

First published in Great Britain in 2006 by
Haus Publishing Limited
26 Cadogan Court
Draycott Avenue
London SW3 3BX

www.hauspublishing.co.uk

A CIP catalogue record for this book is available from the British Library

ISBN 1-904950-63-9

Designed by BrillDesign
Typeset in Garamond 3 by MacGuru Ltd
info@macguru.org.uk

Printed and bound by Graphicom, Vicenza

Front cover: John Holder

Contents

Part One: THE LIFE
Chapter 1: Young Imperialist in a Hurry, 1874–1900   1
Chapter 2: Imperialism, Social Reform and War,
               1900–22   22
Chapter 3: In Defence of the British Empire and the
               Constitution, 1922–40   51

Part Two: THE LEADERSHIP
Chapter 4: The British Empire Alone, 1940–1   69
Chapter 5: Grand Alliance but Gradual Decline, 1941–5   85
Chapter 6: Cold War and the End of Empire, 1945–65   101

Part Three: THE LEGACY
Chapter 7: Churchill's Premiership in Perspective   123

Notes   132
Chronology   147
Further Reading   154
Picture Sources   158
Index   160

Part One

THE LIFE

Chapter 1: Young Imperialist in a Hurry, 1874–1900

Winston Leonard Spencer-Churchill was born at Blenheim Palace at 1.30 a.m. on 30 November 1874. His mother, the former Jennie Jerome, was American. His father, Lord Randolph Henry Spencer-Churchill, was the younger son of the seventh Duke of Marlborough. She was then 20 and he was 25.

It was still an age when to be an aristocrat was a major advantage in British politics and in families such as Winston's there was a pattern of political activity. Conservative and Liberal governments alike had places for numerous peers. Benjamin Disraeli, who was Conservative Prime Minister in 1868 and 1874–80, often eulogised the role of the House of Lords and the monarchy in the British political system, idealising in particular the landed interest. He liked to include major aristocrats in his governments and he greatly enjoyed their company. John Winston Spencer-Churchill, the seventh Duke of Marlborough, was one of these peers. He served as Lord President of the Council in 1867–8 and Lord Lieutenant of Ireland in 1876–80. Disraeli considered the Duke to have 'culture, intellectual grasp and moral energy'.[1] The young Winston's earliest memories were of Dublin, where his father acted as secretary to the Duke.

Lord Randolph Churchill entered Parliament after the

1874 general election. He was returned for Woodstock, a seat greatly under the family's influence and which had earlier been occupied by his father. Lord Randolph's maiden speech in the House of Commons was praised by Disraeli. He wrote to the Queen that Churchill captivated his audience 'by his energy, and natural flow, and his impressive manner'.[2] Lord Randolph, although not hesitating on occasion to annoy Disraeli, took up his rhetoric of social reform and called it 'Tory Democracy', especially after the statesman's death in 1881. Winston, when writing his biography of his father, was to make him more principled and consistent than was the case. Lord Randolph in fact fluctuated between the rhetoric of social reform and adopting markedly illiberal poses. Winston also was to invoke Disraeli both early in his political career and when trying to revive Conservative support after 1945. Although Winston never met Disraeli, he enjoyed working at Chartwell on an upright desk that had belonged to him.

Winston's mother was born in January 1854 in Brooklyn, New York, the daughter of Leonard Jerome who (according to his daughter) made and unmade several fortunes. Jeanette (known as Jennie) Jerome and her two sisters were educated in Paris between 1867 and 1870, and then London. She met Lord Randolph at a society dance on HMS *Ariadne* at Cowes on 12 August 1873 and they became engaged that week. They were married on 15 April 1874, after a long wrangle between their fathers over the details of the marriage settlement. Although theirs was a passionate love relationship, within ten years they went their own ways but within the marriage. Her world was that of high society, his became politics. Winston was born prematurely seven and a half months after their marriage, when Lady Randolph was visiting Blenheim, although possibly his conception had occurred when they were engaged, not married. On 4 February 1880 she gave birth to a second son, John Strange (known as Jack). He became a stockbroker, and died in 1947.

Winston Churchill, like most children of the upper classes, saw more of his nanny than his mother, who enjoyed the social season and the pastimes of the upper classes. Of his mother he later recalled, *My picture of her in Ireland is in a riding habit, fitting like a skin and often beautifully spotted with mud.* To him, she seemed *a fairy princess.*[3] In contrast, Mrs Elizabeth Ann Everest, his nanny, was down-to-earth and gave him the love and attention he craved as and when he wanted it and was almost ever-present. He imbibed her popular Protestantism and displayed it at school, rebelling against ritual in the form of genuflecting to the east during a school service in the Chapel Royal, and later in extolling a form of patriotic Protestantism in his historical writings. He also warmed to her enthusiasm for her native county of Kent, later commenting that as a result he thereafter wanted to live in the county. When he could buy a substantial home of his own in 1922, it was Chartwell Manor, near Westerham in Kent.

The young Winston accompanied Mrs Everest to stay with her sister, Mrs Balaam, at 2 Verona Cottages, Ventnor on the Isle of Wight several times, going with his younger brother on the later occasions. One incident which stayed with him for the rest of his life occurred there on 24 March 1878. Out walking on the cliffs, they saw the *Eurydice* sailing by, a training ship on its return from the West Indies. Storm clouds sent them scurrying home, but the squall resulted in the ship foundering with all but two of some 334 men drowning. On their next walk along the cliffs they joined crowds looking at where three masts were sticking up out of the water.[4] This disaster appears to have been absorbed with fatalism by the growing boy. Perhaps Mrs Everest impressed on him the mystery of God's ways or the popular fatalism of

'When your number is up, it is up and there is nothing you can do about it'. The young Churchill certainly developed a faith in his destiny, having confidence when in dangerous situations that Divine Providence would spare him for some great purpose. Indeed, when he reflected on God in *My Early Life* in 1930 he came near to suggesting that his faith in God hinged on his belief God had favoured him on many occasions. Perhaps this was a milder version of W E Gladstone's view of his relationship with the Almighty.

While Mrs Everest was his closest emotional support for his first 20 years, he still sought the love and approval of his parents. Lady Randolph Churchill busied herself in Society, even being favoured by the Prince of Wales (the future King Edward VII). Lord Randolph's life focused heavily on politics in the 1880s, with him providing with a few colleagues ('the Fourth Party') a vigorous opposition to Gladstone, from 1880 to 1885, and then occupying high office as Secretary of State for India (1885–6) and Chancellor of the Exchequer (1886), before committing political suicide by a rash resignation. Winston's early letters to his father were filled with requests to his father to visit him. Lord Randolph cared for his son more than Winston probably discerned, and quite possibly the more Winston demanded attention, the more it convinced his father he should not mollycoddle his son. Yet Winston was to combine a powerful need for attention and affection with drive and bravery, as his first quarter-century in particular showed.

His self-centredness and his determination to achieve, indeed his apparent need to overachieve, were linked to his craving for attention. These traits were reinforced by his belief in his class's and his family's inherited right to pre-eminence in politics, the army and other traditional aristocratic spheres of influence. His political career was much helped by his aristocratic background, just as was that of Arthur Balfour, Prime Minister 1902–5, who was the nephew of Lord Salisbury. However, his younger brother Jack was very different, not sharing these characteristics in spite of being from the same background. In contrast, a notably similar overachiever was David Lloyd George but he was of a markedly different social background. He was from humble origins, a 'cottage bred' person as he liked to emphasise. Yet he too sought attention and approval, in his case from his uncle, Richard Lloyd, who with his mother brought him up. Like Winston Churchill, he had a self-effacing brother; in Lloyd George's case his brother William's selfless hard work in their solicitors' practice enabled him to enter politics. The Churchill and Lloyd George comparison is also close in their approach to marriage partners, both being breathtakingly blunt to the women whom they were to marry that they would take second place to their political careers. Hence, Churchill's social background explains his early confidence that in due course he would have a political career and it assisted him in his pushing himself forward. However, it does not explain his need to achieve public prominence, which stems more from his feelings of insecurity with his parents and other deeply individual traits.

One of the oddest features of Churchill's early years was his very mixed record at school. For one who desperately sought his parents' approval, he was notably wayward in learning at his first school, St George's, Ascot. He went there from nearly eight until he was four months short of ten, November 1882 to July 1884. He rebelled against the discipline and was repeatedly beaten. He appears often to have displayed a high degree of stubbornness, refusing to learn what did not interest him and being resentful at leaving his parents and Mrs Everest. His school report at the end of his first term noted his weakness in mathematics, with the second term's report commenting, 'Could do better than he does', though later he improved. In contrast, with history and geography, which caught his imagination, he was often very good. In all this he was not an untypical school child, yet it was a contrast with the outstanding ability he later showed. The headmaster of St George's even observed, 'He has no ambition'.[5]

His parents appear to have disapproved of the brutal discipline at St George's and also worried about his health, so they moved him to a more kindly regime under Miss Charlotte and Miss Kate Thomson, then fairly elderly women. The choice of school was also intended to boost Winston's health. The school at 29–30 Brunswick Road, Hove, was close to the sea and it was also close to the family's distinguished doctor, Dr Robson Roose.[6] While at school in the Brighton area Winston enjoyed swimming and riding. However, in December 1884 another boy stabbed him in the chest with a penknife, causing a quarter-inch deep wound, when Winston apparently was teasing him and pulling his ears.[7] Dr Roose was also summoned for a more serious matter in March 1886 when Winston was seriously ill with pneumonia. For five days there were very real fears that he might not survive. Roose came to the rescue again at the end of 1887, when Lord and Lady Randolph Churchill were away and Mrs Everest became seriously ill with diphtheria. He took Winston and Jack into his own home, until they were taken to Blenheim Palace by their grandmother, and successfully treated Mrs Everest.

Winston's happy time at Hove ended with him studying in preparation for the entrance examinations to Harrow. As Charlotte Thomson informed his father, Winston 'only scraped through' and, after leaving Harrow 'had a severe attack of sickness'.[8] Harrow was favoured over Eton, Lord Randolph's school, because of its healthier location. Winston went to Harrow in April 1888. While he again failed to excel overall in his studies, at Harrow he developed his existing interest in history and English literature. He had read beyond his age group, and had greatly enjoyed a copy of Robert Louis Stevenson's *Treasure Island* (1883) in early 1884, which his father had given him while still at St George's, Ascot, and later Shakespeare. As he was in the bottom group at Harrow he learned English, not classics. In *My Early Life*

I got into my bones the essential structure of the ordinary British sentence – which is a noble thing.

CHURCHILL

(1930) he paid a fulsome tribute to his English master, Robert Somervell. Through him, he wrote, *I got into my bones the essential structure of the ordinary British sentence – which is a noble thing.*[9] He utilised his impressive memory in June 1888 to win a prize given to all those who could recite without a mistake 1,200 lines of Thomas Babington Macaulay's 'Lays of Ancient Rome'. In October he was less successful when reciting Shakespeare in a competition for a prize. His ability to memorise was to prove valuable later when he delivered pre-prepared speeches without notes.

As at Ascot, Winston underperformed. His first housemaster at Harrow reported to Lady Randolph, 'As far as ability goes he ought to be at the top of his form, whereas he is at the bottom'. However, he did add, after a list of complaints, praise for some of his work in history. Winston won a prize in this subject. The headmaster, the Rev. J E C Welldon, also acknowledged that Winston 'has some great gifts'. Churchill traded his gifts in English composition for an older boy's skill in Latin. In 1930 he recalled of composing essays for his friend: *I used to walk up and down the room dictating – just as I do now.*[10]

At Harrow he found excitement and enjoyment in the

Harrow School Rifle Volunteer Corps. He was a good shot. In May 1888 he took part in a battle with Haileybury's Corps, reporting to his mother, *It was most exciting[,] you could see through the smoke the enemy getting nearer and nearer*. In March the following year he sent his father a detailed plan of manoeuvres at Aldershot. The young Winston also dreamed of military battles while playing with his huge collection of toy soldiers and when writing an 18,000-word essay in 1889 on an imaginary battle between British and Russian forces in the Ukraine.[11] Lord Randolph had a shrewd idea of his son's interests and weaknesses and rightly saw a career in the army as more realistic than as a barrister. So in September 1889 he went into Harrow's army class which Welldon had instituted soon after being appointed as headmaster in 1885. This class prepared students for the entrance examinations to the Royal Military College at Sandhurst.

Winston realised his need to succeed in getting into Sandhurst if he was to avoid a humdrum job in commerce. He first looked to ways to avoid exams, such as entering the army via the militia. However, by this time entrance to Sandhurst was by merit, not aristocratic influence, by this time and he had to compete in spite of his fear of exams making him literally sick. In the preliminary exams he was able to opt to write an English essay, choosing the American Civil War from a choice of three, and not take Latin. However, when he took the main entrance exams in July and November 1892 he failed both times, though improving markedly the second time. As a result Lord Randolph removed him from Harrow to a 'crammer' run by Captain W H James at 5 Lexham Gardens, London. Winston nevertheless continued to display arrogance towards studying. After his first failure Welldon had told him that on his return to Harrow it was essential for him 'to work not by fits and starts but with regular persistent industry'. In March 1893, not long after his start at the crammer, Captain James complained to Lord Randolph of his 'casual manner':

'I think the boy means well but he is distinctly inclined to be inattentive and to think too much of his abilities ... he has been rather too much inclined up to the present to teach his instructors instead of endeavouring to learn from them ... I may give as an instance that he suggested to me that his knowledge of history was such that he did not want any more teaching in it!'

In June he passed at the third attempt, but not sufficiently well to secure an infantry cadetship. Lord Randolph, who would need to find a further £200 per annum to fund him for the cavalry, saw this as a poor return for 'all the advantages you had' and was the result of 'your slovenly happy-go-lucky harum scarum style of work for which you have always been distinguished at your different schools'.[12] In the event, as a result of the withdrawal of others, he was given an infantry cadetship, to the relief of his father. He arrived at Sandhurst in September 1893.

However, at Sandhurst his greatest joy was in riding. Small of stature, he even referred to himself as a pygmy. He was five feet six and seven-tenths inches tall and not robust. In these circumstances a cavalry regiment suited his physique best. At Sandhurst he developed his existing riding skills under its tough training exercises and from 1895 developed a great love for playing polo. With the tacit support of his mother he set out to evade his father's plans for him to join the 60th Rifles, an infantry regiment, and made contact with Colonel John Brabazon, of the 4th Queen's Own Hussars, a family friend. His father's final letter to him in August 1894 told him that while he was alive and Winston was dependent on him, he could forget joining a cavalry regiment. However, Lord Randolph died on 24 January 1895 and within a fortnight Lady Randolph had assisted her son to transfer to the cavalry regiment with effect from 20 February 1895. Like Lady Randolph, Colonel John Brabazon was a major figure in London Society and was one of the Prince of Wales' circle. This was the first of many instances where influence was mobilised to get Winston an advantage not available to others lacking high society connections.

In the years before his departure to India in 1896 the short and slight Churchill appears to have overcompensated for his size in his efforts to secure acceptance by other males of his age group. He had come badly unstuck at the age of 18 in January 1893, showing off as if a hero of contemporary or classical tales by jumping from a bridge into a tree to escape capture by his brother and cousin. The resulting 29-foot fall saw him badly injured and delayed his start at the crammer. Two years earlier, in May 1891 while at Harrow, he was one of two boys caught, out of five, who vandalised windows in a derelict factory. At Sandhurst in November 1894, he was the leading light of a group of hearties who smashed up partitions which had been put up in the interests of temperance and morality between the bars from the auditorium at the Empire Theatre, a place Lord Randolph had earlier taken him. In the 4th Hussars he was associated with bullying and possibly with the rigging of a horse race in which he was a rider in March 1895. He was cleared of wrong-doing with regard to the horse race but that apart, his 'laddish' misdeeds, although unpleasant in the bullying, were not unusual among boys and young men of his age in their pursuit of proof of their manliness. His determination to see military action and to be brave under fire was an extension of his deep need to win approval and even acclaim.

With two and a half months leave due to him in late 1895, Winston Churchill sought an opportunity to experience war. Cuba appealed, not least as he linked it with the pirates of the era of *Treasure Island*. In order to witness Spanish forces repressing Cuban nationalists, he made use of his ample resources of influence. Colonel Brabazon, the British ambassador in Spain (an old political associate of Lord Randolph) and Viscount Wolseley, the Commander-in-Chief of the British Army, were all mobilised to support this 21-year-old junior officer's project. He was in Cuba for nearly three weeks in November–December. The British Army sought the views of Churchill and Reginald Barnes, his fellow officer, on the effectiveness of the Spaniards' rifles and new bullets. The Spanish had their own agenda in allowing Churchill and his companion a guided war tour, the general in Cuba deeming their presence to imply the moral support of Great Britain. The Spanish authorities shrewdly underlined this diplomatic need by awarding Churchill and Barnes a medal each for their 'distinguished comportment' during a military action.[13] Churchill's ambition of being present when shots were fired in war was first achieved on his 21st birthday, in the jungle after Spanish troops had left Arroyo Blanco at the middle of the island.

The Cuba trip also lead to his first journalistic commission, arranged when he was only twenty. He secured from the *Daily Graphic* an offer of five guineas (£5.25) per letter reporting from the front. Again, he owed this to his family connections, his father having written for that newspaper when in South Africa in 1891. Cuba had been briefly under British rule in 1762–3 and as an enthusiast for the British Empire Churchill wrote at the end of his fifth and final newspaper letter, *It may be that future years will see the island as it would be now, had England never lost it – a Cuba free and prosperous, under just laws and a patriotic administration, throwing open her ports to the commerce of the world, sending her ponies to Hurlingham and her cricketers to Lord's, exchanging the cigars of Havana for the cottons of Lancashire, and the sugars of Matanzas for the cutlery of Sheffield.* Mixing with aristocratic Spanish officers he had come to warm to the Spanish case, though by 1898 he was speaking in favour of the US annexing Cuba. In his later reflections, in 1930, he was frank about his insular views of the time. *They felt about Cuba, it seemed, just as we felt about Ireland. This impressed me much. I thought it rather cheek that these foreigners should have the same views and use the same sort of language about their country and their colonies as if they were British.*[14]

The other particularly notable aspect of Churchill's war tourism trip to Cuba was his first visit to the United States on the way. His mother arranged that he and Barnes should stay in New York with one of her friends, William Bourke Cochran (1854–1923), a lawyer and a Democratic member of Congress. Bourke Cochran greatly impressed Churchill then and later. In an article in the *Strand* magazine in 1931 Churchill placed him second to Lord Randolph as an influence on him and in a letter to his wife in 1909 he observed that Bourke Cochran was *perhaps the finest orator in America ... and a mind that has influenced my thought in more than one important direction.* This was in reinforcing his faith in Free Trade, a decisive issue in Churchill's early political career. Churchill was to quote with approval *words which I learned fifty years ago from a great Irish-American orator* when he made his famous 'Iron Curtain' speech at Fulton, Missouri, on 5 March 1946.[15]

On their first meeting in 1895 Bourke Cochran reinforced Churchill's existing belief that his future lay in taking up the political mantle of his father. A little later, in 1896, the

American predicted that Churchill, if he secured a background of wider social science reading, 'would take a commanding position in public life'.[16] Churchill himself had been eager to emulate the political career of his father. He had seen himself initially buttressing his father in the way that Herbert Gladstone and Austen Chamberlain did their fathers. In *My Early Life* (1930), he even commented of Lord Randolph, *Had he lived another four or five years, he could not have done without me.* Before going to Cuba Churchill was already growing restless at the slack time in a military career, and was using his leisure hours to read his father's speeches and great historical works by Edward Gibbon and William Lecky, as he did more extensively the following year when stationed at Bangalore. In August 1895 he had confided in his mother that he did not feel that the army would suit him for long. *It is a fine game to play – the game of politics – and it is well worth waiting for a good hand before plunging.*[17]

Young Winston's wars were a means to acquiring such a good hand. As Churchill wore his ambition on his sleeve and was breathtakingly honest, his eventual political aspirations were reasonably well-known. Hence, it was not only Churchill's persistent use of influence to get himself preferential treatment to get into action that made him unpopular but also the growing awareness that he was wanting this not to advance a military career but a political one. While in India he began predicting to people that one day he would be Prime Minister. Over 30 years later, when he wrote *My Early Life*, he still did not understand why his behaviour caused so much resentment. After commenting on those who diligently did the routine work without clamouring to be prioritised for a taste of glory, he wrote, with a touch of irony, *Others proceeded to be actually abusive, and the expressions 'Medal-hunter' and 'Self-advertiser' were used from time to time in some high and some low military circles in a manner which would, I am sure, surprise and pain the reader of these notes. It is melancholy to be forced to record these less amiable aspects of human nature, which by a most curious and indeed unaccountable coincidence have always seemed to present themselves in the wake of my innocent footsteps, and even sometimes across the path on which I wished to proceed.*[18] That the less amiable human beings were not misguided in their assessment is borne out by one of his letters of mid-1896 to Lady Randolph. At a time when Churchill was seeking to see action in Crete, the Sudan or Matebeland (now in Zimbabwe), he wrote, *A few months in South Africa would earn me the SA medal and in all probability the company's Star. Thence hot foot to Egypt – to return with two more decorations in a year or two – and beat my sword into an iron despatch box.*[19]

After Cuba, he successfully mobilised all the influence he could muster to get himself present for military engagements at Malakand and Tirah (on the Indian frontier), the Sudan and South Africa. When the 4th Hussars were based at Hounslow barracks before departing for India, Churchill lived with his mother and went to many Society events. He met General Sir Bindon Blood at the home of Lord William Beresford and 'extracted' (as he himself put it) a promise of a place if Blood made a further military expedition to the Malakand Pass.

In the event his joining Blood's forces (which he did from 3 September to 12 October 1897) depended on him being the correspondent for a major newspaper. Earlier, in June 1896, he had secured a *Daily Chronicle* commission of £10 a letter as Special Correspondent if he got to Crete. His mother, to his wrath, only secured £5 a letter from the *Daily Telegraph*, but he was also being paid as war correspondent of the *Pioneer* newspaper, Calcutta. He had favoured the London publication of his letters being signed, in order to further his political career. The 15 letters appeared as 'by a young officer', but Lady Randolph made sure those in London Society knew the identity of the author.[20]

Churchill saw action and displayed bravery under fire. In the Mamund Valley, Churchill was with Sikh troops when they were attacked by an overwhelming number of Pathans. He steadied the retreat, until the East Kent Regiment advanced, saving the day. The distinguished military historian Sir John Keegan has speculated that this action helped to confirm Churchill's belief in the British right to rule in India.[21] Be this as it may, as a result of this action on 16 September 1897, he was mentioned in despatches by Blood: Brigadier-General Jeffreys 'has praised the courage and resolution of Lieutenant W.L.S. Churchill, 4th Hussars, the correspondent of the *Pioneer* newspaper with the force, who made himself useful at a critical point'. He confided in his mother, *I do not suppose any honour or dignity which it may be my fortune in life to deserve or receive will give me equal pleasure.*[22] To this honour was added the India Medal.

After his five weeks or so with the Malakand Field Force he was very eager to publish a book about it, and to get it out before one by Lord Fincastle, the *Times'* correspondent. Earlier, following in the footsteps of Disraeli, Churchill had begun writing an adventure story entitled *Savrola* (published in 1900). Disraeli had written in 1834 to his sister, 'I must publish yet more, before the attention which I require can be obtained'. Churchill, who had denied he intended writing a book on his Cuban adventures, put much effort into *The Story of the Malakand Field Force* (1898). He was delighted by a review in the *Athenaeum* which observed that 'it suggests in style a volume by Disraeli', with the influence of Edmund Burke's style also apparent.

Churchill's first book was a lucid, even gripping, account of frontier warfare. While the book records true bravery of a very high order, it nevertheless has in places the flavour of boys' own adventure yarns. Perhaps this is not surprising given the heroics at Chakdara, where seven defenders were killed and it was believed that the attackers lost over 2,000 men. Churchill, in writing it, delighted in giving it the flavour of a regimental history, earnestly providing roll calls of honour, with full details of British officers but only the numbers of casualties in the 'Native Ranks'. The tone of the book is precocious, with passages of wisdom, probably intended to be in the manner of Gibbon and Macaulay. The 23-year-old author offered his considered opinions on the role of British cavalry officers and men in India and also on political advisers as well as the lessons to be drawn from the campaigns he describes. His comments on the commanding officer, Sir Bindon Blood, were maladroit while he was mildly disparaging about Lord Elgin, Viceroy of India, who would be his future chief at the Colonial Office. Not surprisingly he was viewed as bumptious by some higher-ranking officers.

The book, like his letters to the *Daily Telegraph*, exuded pride in empire. He presumed shared values between author and readers: support for a 'Forward policy' at the edges of the Empire, unquestioning belief in the glory of dying bravely for Queen and country and a ready acceptance of, even a delight in, high casualties inflicted on the enemy. Some of the attitudes in the book are very much of the time and less acceptable now; not least the approval alike of Sir Bindon Blood's prowess at big game hunting (30 tigers with his own rifle) and the bayoneting of 30 brave tribesmen holding a hospital building at Chakdara (*a finish in style*).

After the excitement of the Malakand expedition, Churchill mobilised his influence to join Sir William Lockhart on another North-West Frontier campaign to the Tirah Maidan. He recalled of his mother, *In my interest she left no wire unpulled, no stone unturned, no cutlet uncooked. Under my direction she had laid vigorous siege both to Lord Wolseley and Lord Roberts.*[23] The various wire pulling worked. He was assigned to Sir William but peace prevailed in the area.

So, Churchill focused his attention on joining Kitchener's campaign in the Sudan, yet again exerting maximum influence. Even Lord Salisbury, the Prime Minister and his father's political nemesis, was prevailed on to give support. Kitchener repeatedly made clear that he would not privilege Churchill over those with greater claims. Eventually he evaded Kitchener's veto by being appointed by the War Office, again succeeding in this through his family's social connections. For this campaign he arranged to write for the *Morning Post*, at £15 a letter. As a result he took part in one of the greatest of Victorian imperial battles, Omdurman, on 2 September 1898. Before the battle, he reported direct to Kitchener on the speed and size of the advancing Dervish army. During the later stages he participated in one of the last great cavalry charges. The 21st Lancers, a body of 310 men, charged a force of some 3,000 dervishes who were between the main battle-field and Khartoum. He wrote to his mother two days later, *The charge was nothing as alarming as the retirement on the 16th of Sept last year. It passed like a dream and some part I cannot quite recall.* Characteristically, in the same letter he informed her of his plans which were already underway to write a book of the campaign. He was subsequently awarded the Queen's Sudan Medal and the Khedive's Sudan Medal.

His second book, *The River War*, published in November 1899, was a major achievement, not least for a person in their mid-twenties. It is written in fine style, without the more blatant straining for effect of his first book. He successfully injected tension and varied pace into his narrative. He again drew on the styles of Gibbon and Macaulay. Like his earlier book it is often exciting to read. It benefits from details he gained from the Director of Military Information, from oral testimony and from his own eyewitness accounts. In it he thrust himself to near centre-stage for the climax of the two-volume book. As with his earlier book, *The River War* was something of a paean to British imperialism. After due reflection on the terrible loss of life, including of *the valiant Arabs*, he concluded that *it may be stated in all seriousness that English history does not record any instance of so great a national satisfaction being more cheaply obtained*. The book contained much English racial superiority. Gordon, for instance, inspired *soldiers of inferior race*. The negroes of the Sudan were dismissed as having *the virtues of barbarism*, while the *smallness of their intelligence excused the degradation of their habits*. And yet alongside much of this type of thing there was a degree of respect for the Mahdi and his faith, with Churchill predicting

In the Sudan campaign, Churchill served with several men who would go on to play major roles in his later career. The commander-in-chief, Lord Kitchener, was to be Secretary of State for War while Churchill was First Lord of the Admiralty 1914–15, Captain Douglas Haig, attached to the Egyptian cavalry, was to be Commander-in-Chief of the BEF 1915–19, and Lieutenant David Beatty, who threw Churchill a bottle of champagne from his gunboat, was Churchill's Naval Secretary at the Admiralty in 1911 and went on to command first the Battle Cruiser Fleet and then the Grand Fleet in the First World War.

of the Sudan that *the first Arab historian who shall investigate the early annals of that new nation will not forget, foremost among the heroes of his race, to write the name of Mohammed Ahmed.*[24] Churchill did respect his Arab adversaries in war, and was genuinely disgusted by Kitchener's desecration of the Mahdi's tomb at Khartoum.

After the Sudan campaign Churchill turned away from the army to seek public acclaim through politics and journalism. He put in his resignation from his army commission in January 1899 and he was formally gazetted out on 3 May. His final imperial adventure was in South Africa, again going on behalf of the *Morning Post*. After the high quality of his despatches from the Sudan, he was able to negotiate £1,000 for four months' work as war correspondent for that paper, with £200 a month thereafter. Eager to be close to the action Churchill went up the coast from Cape Town to Durban and then by train to Pietermaritzburg. Thwarted from going to Ladysmith because it was besieged, he eagerly went on an armoured train between Estcourt and Chieveley to assess the Boer advance. In the resulting ambush of the train Churchill displayed conspicuous bravery in ensuring the escape of the railway engine and the wounded, but was captured by Louis Botha, the future President of South Africa, and marched to Pretoria. Churchill escaped captivity on 12 December and, against all odds, made his way to Laurenco Marques and from there by steamship back to Durban, arriving on 23 December. The Boers had offered a 'dead or alive' reward of £25 for his capture. His safe arrival, at a time when the war was going very badly for Britain, was celebrated as if it was a military victory.

Churchill asked the British commander Sir Redvers Buller for a commission, and this was agreed but with no pay, given his unwillingness to give up his journalism for the *Morning Post*. So he rejoined the army as a lieutenant in the South

African Light Horse, serving from 2 January to 29 March 1900, but still holding his commission to that July. He observed the Battle of Spion Kop, even taking a message to the commanding officer on the summit, and he was involved in the fighting which preceded the relief of Ladysmith on 3 March 1900. From April, he accompanied troops again as a war correspondent, an arrangement initially blocked by Lord Roberts and Lord Kitchener, both of whom resented past criticism of the army by Churchill, but with Roberts giving way, as he put it 'for your father's sake' (Lord Randolph having been a friend).[25] He was among the first to enter Pretoria on 5 June 1900 and he and his cousin secured the surrender of the Boer troops at the prisoner of war camp. As was his wont, he put his life at risk and displayed further conspicuous bravery in the period he was a war correspondent until his departure on 7 July 1900. The following year he received the Queen's South Africa Medal, with six clasps, for his participation in the campaigns but as his most notably bravery had been as a war correspondent he did not gain medals for his gallantry.

He published his despatches to the *Morning Post* in two books, *London To Ladysmith, Via Pretoria* (May 1900) published with an illustration of the armoured train in the veldt printed on its cover, and *Ian Hamilton's March* (October 1900). Unlike his two earlier books, these were mostly reprints of his newspaper despatches. His introductory note to the first was written in Durban on 10 March 1900 at the same time as the last despatch in the book on the relief of Ladysmith a week earlier. Highly topical, the book had quickly sold 11,000 copies in Britain before he left South Africa.

So, the fame that he had sought before a parliamentary career was his. He had hoped for medals, and by 1901 he had four, from India, the Sudan and South Africa (as well as one from Spain, with another given later). He had sought to draw attention to himself, as his father had done, by journalism and then by publishing such work in book form. In this he had surpassed his father, writing with a brilliance surprising for his age. Lord Randolph had famously referred to Gladstone in June 1886 as 'an old man in a hurry'. His son in the last years of the 19th century was very much a young imperialist in a hurry. He continued his rush to fame as a politician in the next decade and a half.

Chapter 2: Imperialism, Social Reform and War, 1900–22

Winston Churchill's political career began in the ashes of that of his father. His early political motivation was to ensure that his father's issues and concerns would rise phoenix-like and dominate British politics. His father's career overshadowed his for just a few years, from the late 1890s to when he switched parties in May 1904. Yet, as Robert Rhodes James and Roy Foster have argued, Lord Randolph's career was manipulated by the young Winston to justify his own.[1]

The popular images of Lord Randolph were of a charismatic aristocrat with great abilities marred by a flightiness of purpose, a great egotist yet an Icarus of politics, whose own actions brought about his destruction. Winston wrote of his father, *He possessed the strange quality, unconsciously exerted and not by any means to be stimulated, of compelling attention, and of getting himself talked about.* Winston had also this quality, though in his case it was achieved by very hard work. While others saw Lord Randolph's career as a terrible warning, Winston saw it as noble and took to sounding and acting like his father. In so doing he unintentionally began his career by encouraging doubts about his reliability and judgement. The political legacy of Lord Randolph was a poisoned chalice and eventually his son came to realise that his father's destruction was not primarily due to the unprovoked malice of others.[2]

Thus Winston Churchill's political career began in a passionate desire to vindicate his father's reputation and to carry on what he believed to be his father's legacy. His statements of this legacy were, in fact, strange constructs which recast his father's responses to the needs of the moment into a coherent, altruistic and principled political creed. The father, who was so often too busy to visit him, was provided with noble preoccupations, perhaps thereby justifying in the son's mind his much-felt neglect.

His own identity hinged on his aristocratic pedigree linked to his celebrity parents. As a scion of the Dukes of Marlborough, attention was his due. More than that, his parents were bright stars in the political and social firmaments. As a boy he boosted his pocket money by selling the many autographs he pestered his parents to send him. He quite literally traded on their names. In writing the biography of his father he undertook both a labour of love and a career move. He had written *The Malakand Field Force* in three months, *The River War* in nine months and was still speedy, given the scale of the work and the large collection of his father's papers, in completing *Lord Randolph Churchill* in just over three years, from August 1902 until October 1905. He mobilised his brother Jack to help sort and select correspondence for him. From the outset he saw his father's career as *a great and vivid drama*, as he put it to his mother. However, as well as making his father a tragic hero, Lord Randolph's career was remoulded so as to give it greater consistency and a more 'Tory democracy' and so more liberal a bias. After changing parties, as he did in May 1904, the younger Churchill revealed in two large volumes of pious biography that he was going where his father would have gone had he lived longer. More than that, his father had linked his Conservatism to the needs of the urban population; and in rejecting Free Trade and the other concerns of working people the Conservatives, not Winston Churchill, had deviated from Lord Randolph's wisdom. For a while, Churchill *abandoned politics for literature* (as he wrote in September 1904) to establish the legacy, if not the legend, of Lord Randolph, just as the Liberal politician John Morley, who encouraged him in his biographical task, had taken time out from Liberal Party politics to commemorate William Ewart Gladstone in three substantial volumes, published in 1903. Churchill used his version of the legacy of Lord Randolph in current politics, just as the various Liberal leaders wielded the legacy of the dead Gladstone in pursuit of their own political advantage. Winston Churchill was further encouraged in his biographical endeavours by Morley's talk of him earning the then huge amount of £8,000 to £10,000, the lower sum being realised.[3]

He launched his political career in a way which made clear that he was taking up his father's mantle. Lord Randolph had been the principal founder of the Primrose League in 1883, set up to honour Disraeli's career and ideas. Winston had joined the League while at school in 1887. He had written much of 'Tory democracy' to his mother and others. His first public speech, arranged by Conservative Central Office, was at Claverton Manor, Bath, on 26 July 1897. His speech was carefully crafted and it made an up-to-date statement of Tory democracy. In it he claimed that the Conservatives were the true friends of working men, citing what was to be the Workman's Compensation Act 1897, and envisaging a future where profit-sharing in industry would replace the industrial conflict then epitomised by a major engineering lock-out. The resulting cheers and the substantial press reports strengthened his taste for politics.[4]

Yet while his early political views owed a great deal to his father, they also drew on his own endeavours. Lord Randolph had been right in judging his elder son to have squandered much of the best educational opportunities that his money could buy. While no dunce, he had performed well below his abilities. He caught up by self-help in the form of intensive reading and his magpie mind took up glittering ideas from wherever he could find them for the rest of his life. Once he found attractive ideas, he proclaimed them in his lucid and striking prose. As Violet Bonham Carter, one of his oldest friends, later wrote, 'Even the eternal verities appeared to him an exciting personal discovery'.[5]

In his only novel, *Savrola* (1900), he also displayed his early political beliefs. He wrote 80 pages on his journey back to India, soon after his speech at Claverton. He informed his mother, *All my philosophy is put into the mouth of the hero.* Churchill put much of himself into his novel. Among the most striking observations made by his hero were those concerning evolution and empire, an almost didactic statement of Social Darwinism. The following are short extracts from these comments: *Nature never considers the individual; she only looks at the average fitness of the species ... We cannot say that a good man will always overcome a knave; but the evolutionist will not hesitate to affirm that the nation with the higher ideals would succeed ... Evolution does not say 'always' but 'ultimately'. Well, ultimately civilisation has climbed up beyond the reach of barbarism.* He also reflected on European technical supremacy, observing that even when European moral supremacy has gone, *our Maxims* [machine guns] *will remain* and defeat *the valiant savages* who assail them.

Savrola also had an implicit message that aristocrats, real or natural, would effortlessly lead the many. It showed – what David Lloyd George was to see – that Churchill's democratic principles had firm class limitations. In *Savrola* Churchill displayed the upper class's dark fears of violent anarchists and socialists, without perceiving differences between them. In the manner of later novels by John Buchan or 'Sapper' (Cyril McNeile), he had his pantomime extremists. His heroine, Lucile, comes across two men 'of foreign aspect' who speak of 'the idea of a community of wives' as 'part of the great scheme of society'. Here Churchill aired fears that would resurface with the 1917 Bolshevik revolution in Russia. He also gratuitously commented on *the Socialists who, however much they might approve of the application of dynamite to others, did not themselves relish the idea of a personal acquaintance with high explosives*. For good measure, he wrote of an evil German socialist, Kreutze, who he may well have derived from the German Social Democrats' theorist Karl Kautsky. Churchill's ideal working-class figures in his novel included an elderly woman, an old nurse, based on Mrs Everest, of whom he observed that *history does not concern itself with such*. For all his talk of 'Tory Democracy', he was long acquainted with a only narrow range of working people.

Savrola had the merits of some strong writing in the battle scenes, whether on land or at sea. As a novel, which he referred to as 'a political romance', it was in parts like the work of a clever 16-year-old, gauche and, especially early on, lacking in depth.[6] Perhaps, above all, he displayed, as his grandmother told him, a striking lack of understanding of women. His heroine was a Victorian princess figure, idealised and unreal; perhaps, worrying in a man in his mid-twenties (when it was published), Lucile appeared to reflect his image of his mother.

With his first election campaign in June–July 1899, Churchill put 'Tory Democracy' into action, by standing in a double by-election for Oldham, a Lancashire cotton town. Lancashire was a centre of working class Toryism. *I am a Tory Democrat*, he declared early on. *I regard the improvement of the*

condition of the British people as the main aim of modern government.
However, he tempered such sentiments with qualifications
that emphasised that reforms
should not impair the working *The existing order of society is driven by*
of market forces. In Glasgow in *one mainspring – competitive selection. It*
October 1906 he commented, *may be a very imperfect organisation of*
The existing order of society is *society but it is all we have got between us*
driven by one mainspring – com- *and barbarism.*
petitive selection. It may be a very
imperfect organisation of society CHURCHILL
but it is all we have got between us and barbarism.

Oldham was then a two-member seat and Churchill stood
with a trade unionist, James Mawdsley, probably the first
trade unionist that he had ever met. His comments on trade
unionists in *Savrola* suggested he had little understanding
of them. He appears not to have realised that Mawdsley was
a very rare person, a leading trade unionist who was a Conservative. In *My Early Life* he wrote, *The partnership of 'The
Scion and the Socialist' seemed a splendid new orientation in politics*,
yet Mawdsley had distinguished himself at the TUC by being
a notable anti-socialist.[7] Both Churchill and Mawdsley lost.
However, in the 'Khaki' election in September-October 1900
he won one of the seats back for the Conservatives by the
narrow majority of 222 votes. His bravery in South Africa,
added to his first place on the ballot paper and that, unlike
the other Conservative, he had stood before, ensured enough
voters plumped for him when splitting their votes between
the Liberals and Conservatives.

As a Conservative MP Churchill first made his mark by
criticising his own front bench. He exercised his military
knowledge by attacking St John Brodrick's proposals for
army reforms. His attack also represented a further exercise
in filial piety, his father having wrecked his career over

army expenditure in 1886 when Brodrick had been Under-Secretary of State at the War Office. Churchill attacked the proposals on grounds of excessive expenditure which would have little real benefit, suggesting that if there was to be increased expenditure it would be most effectively spent on the navy. In opposing Brodrick's scheme he invoked the names of Disraeli and Lord Salisbury as well as that of his father.[8]

In all this there was a danger that he would be seen as his father's son, emulating Lord Randolph's worst features. There was an aristocratic presumption of easy superiority, an expectation of rapid preferment. Winston Churchill attacked big political figures; but whereas Lord Randolph in his Fourth Party days had attacked Gladstone yet humiliated his own Leader in the House of Commons, his son directly attacked not only Brodrick but Arthur Balfour, Joseph Chamberlain and others. He was already a rebel before he broke with the Conservatives over Chamberlain's desire for tariffs, but this policy was sufficient to cause him to change parties. Churchill strongly supported Free Trade, concurring with Disraeli's comments of mid-century, 'Protectionism is not only dead but damned'. When publishing his speeches on Free Trade in 1906, Churchill made much of Disraeli's views.[9] Clearly, in his early political career his figures of reference were both Lord Randolph and Disraeli.

His career as a Liberal politician in effect began on 23 December 1903 when the General Purposes Committee of the Oldham Conservative Association passed a resolution of no confidence in him and indicating they would not support him at the next election. This was confirmed, with only one dissenter, on 8 January 1904 by a meeting of the main body of the Association, in spite of Churchill pointing out that Balfour had reaffirmed Free Trade on becoming Prime Minister in

1902 and he (Churchill) had stuck to the past fiscal policy of the party. While this was true, he had delighted in being out of step with his leaders over army and other matters. That he had burned his boats with the Conservatives was emphatically illustrated when the House of Commons Conservative leadership and all but a few Free Trade backbenchers walked out when he was making a speech on 29 March 1904. Churchill offered to resign his seat if his constituents so wished, but the Oldham Conservative Association did not want a by-election, so he remained an MP with honour. On 31 May he crossed the floor of the House of Commons, and took a place beside David Lloyd George, where Lord Randolph had sat during his years in opposition.

Many of the main themes of Churchill's career as a Liberal politician took up his earlier concerns. Both before and after the First World War he continued to display and to develop his imperial views. He also went further in social policy, but retained his belief that such reforms should not economically impinge other than very marginally on the free working of market forces. He was also to display his military background in his interest in controlling public forces when Home Secretary. He was also to develop both naval and military policy while First Lord of the Admiralty (1911–15) and Secretary of State for War (1919–21).

When Balfour's government resigned in December 1905, without first facing the electorate, Sir Henry Campbell-Bannerman formed a Liberal administration. He offered Churchill the important post of Financial Secretary to the Treasury, with H H Asquith holding Lord Randolph's old post of Chancellor of the Exchequer. Churchill persuaded him instead to propose him as Under-Secretary of State for the Colonies. This was second to the post held with distinction by Joseph Chamberlain, who had earlier switched parties. It also had the major attraction of making Churchill the Colonial Office's spokesperson in the House of Commons, Lord Elgin, the Colonial Secretary, being in the House of Lords.

Elgin, then 56, had been Viceroy of India 1894–9, and had chaired a Royal Commission appointed in 1902 to report on the military preparations for the Boer War. A sensible if self-effacing figure, he was a senior politician who patiently tolerated under him the impetuous and decidedly not self-effacing young Churchill on the make. Of the Elgin-Churchill relationship the historian Ronald Hyam has written (overlooking Lloyd George) that 'it was the only one in his political career in which Churchill experienced a restraining hand from above'. Yet, Churchill behaved as if he were a Cabinet minister, not an under-secretary, and often displayed an excess of energy, creating issues and work for the sake of it when underemployed. Hyam concluded that at the Colonial Office his behaviour was 'a curious combination of magisterial statesman and mischievous schoolboy'. Churchill's generous side paid tribute to Elgin's kindness to him and his efficient conduct of business, while his unbridled ambitious side brazenly pressed Asquith for Elgin's job some three weeks before Asquith became Prime Minister, unfairly observing of the Colonial Office that *practically all the constructive action and all the parliamentary exposition has been mine*.[10]

Imperial policy was at the heart of Churchill's interests and, early on, much of the Campbell-Bannerman government's attention was on South Africa in the aftermath of the Boer War. In his new role as the Commons spokesperson for the Colonial Office he got off to a provocative start only three days after the new Parliament met in February 1906 when in a debate on Chinese labour in South Africa he referred to 'the Conservative and Protectionist Party' and raked over the pre-1906 Conservative divisions. His performance a month later, in a debate on a motion of censure on Lord Milner, was judged by many of all parties as at best maladroit, at worst disastrous. Trying to both side with the critics of Milner and yet to give some measure of defence to a civil servant, Churchill succeeded only in sounding – as Margot Asquith put it – 'ungenerous, patronising and tactless'. He indulged in overblown rhetoric, echoing Lord Macaulay on the impeachment of Warren Hastings and gratuitously made comparisons between Charles Stewart Parnell and the Parnell Commission (concerning libellous forgeries) and Milner. Having over-prepared his speech, he failed to gauge the mood of the House and ended up (as Earl Winterton later recalled) 'subdued and crestfallen'.[11] Churchill learned from his mistakes and thereafter was more sensitive to his audience in the House of Commons. Margot Asquith, nevertheless, felt in retrospect, 'Less oratically sensitive than Mr Lloyd George, he is not captivated by his audience, nor does he receive much at any time from his listeners. His words come smoking hot from his mind to his lips and I sometimes think the power of his eloquence would carry on the pageantry of his eloquence even if the entire audience were to disappear.'[12]

> 'His {Churchill's} words come smoking hot from his mind to his lips and I sometimes think the power of his eloquence would carry on the pageantry of his eloquence even if the entire audience were to disappear.'
>
> MARGOT ASQUITH

Churchill was notably constructive in the preparations for returning self-government to the two Boer republics. Even before the 1906 general election he had written a paper calling for a quick resolution of the issue. He worked with Elgin, Asquith, the Lord Chancellor and the Attorney-General to prepare the Transvaal Constitution. In this Churchill secured a more radical settlement than intended by the Conservatives, and he received praise from Lloyd George 'on the way you saved the government from inevitable disaster'.[13] Churchill also made an impact at the sixth Colonial Conference held in London in April 1907. Although not entitled to speak at the conference, Churchill successfully pressed to address it and robustly defended Free Trade. At the associated meetings during the conference he put on the mantle of a statesman (although still only 32) and held forth on the great merits of the British Empire.[14] After the end of the conference, on 1 May 1907, he was made a Privy Councillor, a sign of his continuing political rise.

With the Parliamentary recess in 1907 Churchill put his energies into attending the French army's manoeuvres and then touring East Africa. He went to France with a rising star of the Conservative Party, F E Smith, against whom he had debated at the Oxford Union that March. From October he travelled via Malta, Cyprus and Aden to Mombasa, accompanied by his uncle, Colonel Gordon Wilson, Edward Marsh, his private secretary, and George Scrivings, his long-serving servant. Before leaving he had reverted to his earlier journalistic ways, securing a contract to provide five articles for the *Strand* magazine and a longer account as a book (four-fifths of which was to be the *Strand* pieces), together bringing him £750, enough to fund his travels. Although away from Whitehall, he bombarded government departments with memoranda on the French manoeuvres and then on all manner of aspects of East Africa. On his travels he revelled in being received as if a major government minister. As well as being the subject of numerous welcoming ceremonies, he earnestly saw many deputations of local people. Given his marginal Manchester seat, he made much mention in his articles and book of Manchester and cotton as well as of Manchester settlers in Kenya and he advocated Uganda as rich in potential for investment in cotton plantations. More generally, he wrote on the prospects of imperial economic development, urging that the state promote more railways and hydro-electric power.

As with South Africa, Churchill did not question white people's superiority. Nevertheless, in East Africa he considered the prospects for the Indian population as well as for black Africans. His attitudes remained Victorian, with much earnest urging of the government to assist natives to move towards *civilised attitudes*, away from *primary squalor without religion, without clothes, without morals*, and complaining that the natives had no right to live in idleness but should be industrious. He also boasted of the animals he slaughtered in the name of sport, including three rare white rhinoceroses, other rhinoceroses, a hippopotamus, lions, buffalo, warthogs and antelopes. His journey ended in tragedy when he returned to Khartoum, George Scrivings contracting cholera and dying within 15 hours. His book, *My African Journey*, was published in December 1908, with a print run of 12,500 copies.

Before its publication, Winston Churchill was married. His engagement was longer than that of his parents, but only by three weeks. Unlike David Lloyd George, Churchill was not a great success with women. He was too wrapped up in himself to think of their interests and concerns. His small talk was of himself, his achievements and his ambitions, often more a monologue than a conversation. In India in November 1896 he had been attracted to Pamela Plowden, *the most beautiful girl I have ever seen* (as he wrote to his mother). They became friends, with Lady Randolph and others up to 1900 expecting them to marry. Instead she married the Earl of Lytton in 1902 and later commented to Edward Marsh, 'The first time you meet Winston you see all his faults, and the rest of your life you spend in discovering his virtues'.[15] Another female friend, Muriel Wilson, whom he had known since 1895, had joined him, Lionel Rothschild and Lady Helen Vincent on a motoring tour in Italy in summer 1906. He proposed to her, perhaps then, and later to Miss Ethel Barrymore, the actress.

Churchill's fourth and final notable female relationship of his own age group was with Clementine Hozier. They first met at a ball in 1904, but he was tongue-tied. They met again at a dinner party in March 1908 and, after further meetings, he proposed to her at the Greek temple beside the lake at Blenheim Palace on 11 August. She accepted, but had second thoughts (as she had done before, breaking two previous engagements). However, they were both in love and relieved to find that their feelings were reciprocated. Their wedding day was 12 September 1908. She gave him the emotional stability he needed and she restrained, or lessened, his overbearing tendency and his financial irresponsibility. For her, he was a kind, generous and loyal partner but one whose relentless, self-centred pursuit of his political ambitions wore her down at times, especially when they reached the usual age of retirement. They had five children, Diana, Randolph, Sarah, Marigold (who died aged two) and Mary.

In 1908 Churchill's career was shooting upwards. He succeeded David Lloyd George as President of the Board of Trade on 12 April, under Asquith's premiership. He declined the Admiralty, as it was held by his uncle, Lord Tweedmouth, and probably, also the Local Government Board. He had taken an interest in social policy from the outset of his career, as a key component of 'Tory Democracy', he wrote for T P O'Connor's weekly journal a review of

Upton Sinclair's *The Jungle* (1906), an exposé of the appalling working conditions in the Chicago meatpacking industry, and he helped Charles Masterman, a Liberal MP and an able writer on social problems, with an article for the *Daily News* in September 1907. Moreover, he had displayed Social Darwinism in *Savrola* and by the early years of the 20th century he was speaking of the need for the state to ensure national minimum standards for British people, very much in line with the then current 'national efficiency' ideas of Lord Rosebery, Sidney and Beatrice Webb and others. For a short while his interest in social reform even eclipsed his passion for empire.[16] His period at the Board of Trade was notably innovative and politically potent.

With Lloyd George, he was a major architect of the Liberal social reforms. In 1906 at Glasgow Churchill urged that the state should *spread a net over the abyss,* saying:

> *I do not want to impair the vigour of competition, but we can do much better to mitigate the consequences of failure. We want to draw a line below which we will not allow persons to live and labour yet above which they may compete with all their strength of their manhood.*

He was the major initiator of the measures dealing with unemployment, the setting up of a national system of labour exchanges under the Labour Exchanges Act 1909, and the introduction of unemployment insurance under Part 2 of the National Insurance Act 1911. He also took up the issue of very poorly paid labour with the Trade Boards Act 1909, which fixed minimum wages initially for 200,000 workers of whom 140,000 were female, and was soon extended to more. Churchill was very willing to modify the laws of supply and demand for *what we call sweated trades* for where *you have no organisation, no parity of bargaining, the good employer is undercut by the bad, and the bad employer is undercut by the worst.*[17] Churchill, like Lloyd George before him, was pro-active in trying to resolve industrial disputes. In particular he tried to secure a new sliding agreement in the cotton industry. He had much experience of the textile industries as MP for a Manchester constituency from 1906 to 1908, and for Dundee from 1908 to 1922. He also encouraged the spread of boards of conciliation (which were intended to make strikes and lock-outs unnecessary).

With a government reshuffle following the January 1910 general election, Asquith offered Churchill the post of Chief Secretary for Ireland. Churchill asked instead for either the Admiralty or the Home Office. He was given the latter, serving as Home Secretary from 14 February 1910 until 23 October 1911. He made considerable efforts to be a liberal Home Secretary, taking up his predecessor's prison reforms, introducing legislation to improve mining safety and also working conditions (including a half-day-a-week holiday). However, in contrast, he had imbibed some of the then fashionable ideas of eugenics, even writing to Asquith in December 1910 of *the multiplication of the unfit* which he warned was *a very terrible danger to the race.* The Mental Deficiency Act 1913 came after his time and did not go as far as his comments suggest he might have favoured.[18]

However, as so many Home Secretaries have discovered, it is a post likely to bring obloquy on its holder. Churchill succeeded in arousing criticism for appearing to glorify himself in the role of commander of the forces of law and order, as if he were still in the army. On 3 January 1911 he was prominent at Sidney Street in the East End of London when armed police surrounded a house believed to hold members of a gang of anarchists who had committed an armed robbery at a jeweller's shop. He was wrongly accused of taking operational control but he was rightly suspected of greatly enjoying such action. As a result of the siege of Sidney Street he became favourable to tougher restrictions on aliens, something he had opposed in 1904–5, and he introduced a tough Bill in April 1911, which failed through lack of Parliamentary time.

More damaging for his reputation, especially in Wales, was his role in dealing with industrial unrest in Tonypandy, Llanelli and Liverpool in 1910 and 1911. The word 'Tonypandy' was shouted at Churchill in elections for most of the rest of his career, it wrongly being believed miners had been killed there in 1910. In fact, during the very bitter dispute, Churchill and the Secretary of State for War had resisted the local authorities' call for troops, sending instead 800 London police. As in the 1984–5 Miners' Strike, the London police were tougher than the local police and caused bitterness by being none too particular as to whom they batoned. In the case of Liverpool in 1911 Churchill urged the local authorities to use police not troops during unrest but when a national railway strike was called he authorised the use of troops. Lloyd George successfully negotiated a quick ending of the strike. Nevertheless, at Llanelli at the end of the dispute, two people were shot dead by troops when a train was stopped and the engine driver attacked. It was these deaths which were recalled with the shouts of 'Tonypandy'. Yet the Labour movement was right to see Churchill as more a military man than a conciliator, as was to be the case again in the General Strike in 1926. According to Lucy Masterman, Churchill's response to learning that Lloyd George had got the strike called off was, *I'm sorry to hear it. It would have been better to have gone on and given these men a good thrashing.*[19]

From 25 October 1911 Churchill was First Lord of the Admiralty. Earlier, in 1908–9, he had joined Lloyd George in resisting calls to increase immediate building of dreadnought battleships from four to six. With the Agadir crisis of 1911, Churchill and Lloyd George came to see Germany as a danger to Britain. Then the Kaiser, believing France was soon to declare a protectorate over Morocco, sent the gunboat *Panther* to Agadir to overawe the French. Churchill even argued in a memorandum that should Germany make war on France, Britain should join France and Germany be warned of this. In another memorandum of 13 August 1911 he predicted the opening phase of the war that did occur three years later. Churchill's sense of urgency, his pro-active approach and his dynamism as well as Reginald McKenna's failure to insist on the creation of a Naval War Staff caused Asquith to remove McKenna and replace him not with R B Haldane, although he had been a notably effective Secretary of State for War, but with Churchill. Churchill wrote in 1923 that his time at the Admiralty was *the four most memorable years of my life*.[20]

The battlecruiser combined battleship-calibre guns with cruiser speed, though it sacrificed armour protection to achieve it. By 1914 the British had ten such ships, forming the Battle Cruiser Fleet under Sir David Beatty. At Heligoland Bight and the Falklands they proved their superiority over smaller cruisers, but damage at the battle of Dogger Bank in 1915, where they fought their German counterparts, gave a warning of their vulnerability to guns of battleship calibre. At Jutland a year later, three battlecruisers, HMS *Indefatigable*, *Queen Mary* and *Invincible*, were hit by heavy-calibre shells and exploded and sank, there being only a handful of survivors from each.

Churchill was ruthless in purging the Admiralty of those obstructing change, removing the First Sea Lord and three of the four Sea Lords. Churchill, who liked to promote those he knew, had been greatly impressed by Admiral John ('Jackie')

Fisher when they met in the company of King Edward VII at Biarritz in April 1907. Fisher, born in 1841, had been a reforming First Sea Lord, 1904–10, and Churchill made him his unofficial adviser when he pushed through major changes in the navy. In addition to the creation of the Naval War Staff, these changes included building bigger dreadnoughts with heavier guns and a class of fast battlecruisers, arming merchant ships, providing naval aircraft, improving pay and conditions for sailors and speeding up the navy's changeover from coal to oil. As a result of this change of fuel, Churchill had a close association with the British oil industry in 1913–14.[21]

While the North Sea was the vital area, Churchill shared Admiralty concern about the Mediterranean, given both the Austrian and Italian dreadnought fleets. Churchill secured Cabinet approval for a Mediterranean force which could defeat Austria there. However, with the Italians gaining additional naval bases in 1912 and Germany establishing a Mediterranean squadron, Britain helped to modernise the Turkish fleet. Churchill also agreed to Anglo-French naval discussions in July 1912, these leading to an agreement in February 1913. In May 1914 the Cabinet agreed to naval conversations with Russia. With no response to Churchill's offer to Germany in March 1913 of a 'naval holiday', and with Italy building four dreadnoughts, from November 1913 Churchill demanded increased naval construction. This led to a political crisis, with Churchill and the Sea Lords threatening to resign if Lloyd George and the Cabinet did not approve four more dreadnoughts. The situation was resolved in February 1914 with an increase in naval spending over the original estimates.

Churchill was effective and in his element at the Admiralty. He liked dealing with senior Service personnel. Now he could do so as a person of standing, no longer dependent on the influence of his mother or other family members. His past had pointed him in this direction. He had planned his war games with his huge collection of toy soldiers, he had studied war at Sandhurst, he had experienced war and he had written brilliantly of imperial campaigns. Yet for all this, the collapse of his early political career was due to failures which initially arose in his area of expertise.

The First World War began well for Churchill, This was recognised by Kitchener who, when Churchill was leaving the Admiralty, visited him to express his respect for his foresight in having the fleet prepared at the outbreak of war in August 1914. Then Churchill and Prince Louis of Battenberg, the First Sea Lord, had ensured that the First and Third Fleets were in the right places ahead of war and that arrangements had been made for Sir John Jellicoe to take over early as commander-in-chief should war be declared. The naval historian, Vice Admiral Sir Peter Gretton, later gave the verdict that Churchill displayed 'astonishing activity' in the opening months of war and 'took a more active part in the day-to-day running of the war at sea than any First Lord in history'.[22]

Churchill displayed much courage and leadership, but less political sensitivity, in 1914 when he became personally involved in the defence of Antwerp. Kitchener wanted naval artillery and then a Royal Marine Brigade to hold Antwerp in order to delay the German capture of the North Sea coast from there to Calais. Churchill, who had been on his way to Dunkirk, instead went to Antwerp and took charge of the defence for a few days. He undoubtedly stiffened resistance (which continued for four more days after he left on 6 October). One account described him there as being in a naval hat, smoking a large cigar, while shells burst close by. His exploits were denounced by the right-wing press, the *Daily Mail* and the *Morning Chronicle*, and aroused derision from other politicians. Lloyd George commented that he had 'behaved in a rather swaggering way'. There was still something of the Boys' Own hero in his behaviour. This was also true concerning possible spies. While he was alert to national security issues, he could overreact. This was well illustrated when he was travelling by car with naval officers to a remote loch in north-west Scotland. When a searchlight was spotted on Loch Rosque Castle, the home of a Conservative MP, Sir Arthur Bignold, Churchill and others, armed with guns rejected Bignold's explanation that it was used to locate deer for hunting, and put it out of action.[23]

From the outset of the war the navy successfully ensured the transport of men and munitions to France and that the German High Seas Fleet was limited in its movements. Actions off Heligoland Bight on 28 August 1914 and near the Dogger Bank on 23 January 1915 discouraged the German Fleet from venturing into the North Sea in force until 1916. In the South Atlantic at the Battle of Coronel Admiral von Spee defeated a British naval force with heavy losses, but the despatch of two British capital ships resulted in the destruction of all but one of von Spee's force off the Falkland Islands in December 1914. However, probably the worst British naval error of the early part of the war was the German battlecruiser *Goeben* and the light cruiser *Breslau* succeeding in going through the eastern Mediterranean to Constantinople, thereby bringing Turkey into the war.

Churchill's undoing in 1915 arose from his determination to undermine Turkish resolve as a German ally by capitalising on British naval supremacy by getting British and French ships to Constantinople and the Black Sea (where the *Goeben* and *Breslau* were operating). With the Turkish army moving towards Egypt and the Russians asking for British action to relieve Turkish pressure on their forces in the Caucasus,

Kitchener was initially supportive of a purely naval action in the Dardanelles. On 13 January 1915 the War Council decided that the navy should 'bombard and take Gallipoli, with Constantinople as its objective'.

While Churchill was eager, his First Sea Lord, Admiral Lord Fisher, was not. Fisher had returned from retirement on 24 November 1914, after Prince Louis of Battenberg had resigned after being subjected to much anti-German vilification in spite of his patriotic record. Churchill, annoyed that Battenberg had not vigorously supported his Antwerp venture and believing Fisher to be more imaginative, let him go. However, the bringing-back of Fisher was to be a fateful decision. Within a fortnight of the War Council's decision, Fisher became hostile to the Dardanelles campaign, feeling much as Haig did in regard to the army and the Western Front, that British naval strength should not be diluted but maintained in the North Sea. On 4 March 1915 he wrote to Churchill, 'The more I consider the Dardanelles, the less I like it'. Fisher increasingly insisted that further naval resources should not be sent there and, after often threatening to resign, walked out – in spite of pleas from Churchill, Asquith and Lloyd George. The departure of Fisher, along with a press campaign over alleged munitions shortages on the Western Front, provided the occasion for the creation of a coalition government, which included the Conservatives and Labour, in place of the purely Liberal government. It also ended for a time the upward trajectory of Churchill's career. Between Churchill and Fisher there were major policy differences. Churchill could later defend himself over Gallipoli by revealing that Fisher had signed his agreement to all major decisions. Fisher, however, complained that Churchill had overborne him by out-arguing him and that he, Fisher, had made his concerns very clear. An underlying problem was that they were too alike, both highly energetic, opinionated, egotistic and obsessed by their work. For Churchill it proved a fatal mistake to downplay and brush aside Fisher's objections.

Gallipoli was to be a major blot on Churchill's career. While many of the accusations made against him were untrue, nevertheless he had been the most committed supporter of the campaign. Although he had assured the War Council that the navy could succeed on its own, he had continued to back the operation when he came to believe in February that troops were needed. The scale of losses, especially among Australian and New Zealand forces, was to forge stronger national identities through suffering in those countries. In May 1916, Churchill, seeking to restore his reputation, secured Asquith's agreement to publish major documents relating to Gallipoli, but in July Asquith reversed his decision and set up a House of Commons select committee to inquire into the campaign. Churchill spent immense time preparing evidence to vindicate his role and he gave evidence to the commission on 28 September 1916. The resulting report commented that in his evidence Churchill had 'assigned to himself a more unobtrusive part than that which he actually played'. Although the report was mildly critical of Churchill's role, it was not sufficiently so to block the resumption of his career. Later historians, such as Tuvia Ben-Moshe and Robin Prior, have argued that he was not blameless at the operational level, that he should have secured a combined naval and military campaign early on.[24]

One of the conditions that Andrew Bonar Law and the Conservatives made when joining the new Asquith government in May 1915 was that Churchill should leave the Admiralty. Both Lloyd George and Churchill himself pressed Asquith to move him to the Colonial Office, but this post was given to Bonar Law. Churchill was made Chancellor of the Duchy of Lancaster, a post he held from 25 May until 12 November 1915. It was a demotion, but Churchill was appeased by being kept on the War Council (now the Dardanelles Committee). He was still by some ten years the youngest member of the Cabinet. However, when in November Asquith reconstituted the Dardanelles Committee into a smaller war committee, with Churchill excluded, he resigned. Within a week Churchill left for army service on the Western Front. He joined the Guards at Merville for the remainder of 1915. From 1 January 1916 he was in command of the 6th Battalion, Royal Scots Fusiliers, moving into the line at Ploegsteert, in the area of the first battle of Ypres, from 26 January. He again showed bravery and earned the respect of his men. His determination to vindicate his name over Gallipoli and to resume his political activities led him to leave France and to return to London on 9 May 1916.

Over a year later, on 17 July 1917, some four months after the Dardanelles Commission's first report, Lloyd George brought him back into the government as Minister of Munitions, a post he held until January 1919. It was only when there was a political storm over his appointment that Churchill realised the depth of animosity in which he was held by the Conservatives and that Lloyd George had told the truth when he had angered Churchill by saying it was politically impossible to include him in his coalition government when it had been formed in December 1916. Having taken the risk of bringing Churchill in in mid-1917, Lloyd George secured a weighty Liberal Coalitionist to his government, nearly all the other leading Liberals having followed Asquith out of office.

Churchill put energy and political flair into the Ministry of Munitions to an extent not seen there since Lloyd George had been its first minister in 1915–16. While bringing political weight to the ministry, Churchill's worst error there arose from again overriding his officials' advice. In this case he got into a costly mess over wage differentials, his award of a rise to skilled workers leading to substantial unrest by unskilled workers who eventually secured a higher wage settlement.

Nevertheless, for Lloyd George, Churchill was usually a 'safe pair of hands' and when Lord Milner, Secretary of State for War, became discredited in the handling of the demobilisation of soldiers at the end of the war, Churchill succeeded him on 10 January 1919. Churchill recognised that the mutinies among some British troops on both sides of the English Channel were not manifestations of revolutionary sentiments but a desire for a speedy return to civilian life. He acted decisively on this understanding, scrapping the existing demobilisation arrangements and introducing a scheme which was more defensible and closer to the soldiers' interpretation of fair play, which took into account length of service, injuries and age.

Churchill's two years as Secretary of State for War coincided with major demands on military resources in Russia, Ireland, India and Egypt. Churchill was swift to argue that Bolshevik Russia, not Germany, was the major threat. Indeed, his concerns with Bolshevism in Russia and within Britain and his belief that the Third (the Communist) International was effective became near to being obsessional. Churchill's aristocratic background heightened his fear and loathing of revolution. Lloyd George had amused himself before the First World War by teasing Churchill about his inbred hatred of the French Revolution.[25] In 1919 revolution was again spreading through Europe. Basil Thomson, head of Special Branch, recalled three years later, 'In 1919 the word "revolution" was on every lip, as it was in 1793, 1830 and

1848; in 1922 you will hear that the British working man is too staid and sensible a person ever to think of revolution except through the ballot box.' The flames of Churchill's own fears were fanned by Secret Service briefings, which were frequently highly alarmist. While Churchill expressed such fears in 1918–20, Lloyd George was less convinced, declaring to a meeting of Liberals in December 1918, 'Revolution I am not afraid of. Bolshevism I am not afraid of. It is reaction I am afraid of'.[26]

Churchill was the main member of the government who supported Allied intervention in Russia. Lloyd George and the rest of the government were hostile to the Bolsheviks but felt that it was impractical to make a major military intervention, given the war-weariness of Britain, the cost and the unwillingness of the US to countenance it. On 31 December 1918 the War Cabinet agreed to support any government threatened by the Bolsheviks 'in any manner which did not involve military intervention ... and that our general policy should be that ... of walling off a fire in a mine'. In February 1919 Lloyd George commented to Lord Riddell, a press baron and a friend, 'Winston is in Paris. He wants to conduct a war against the Bolsheviks. That *would* cause a revolution! Our people would not permit it.' To Churchill, he telegrammed, 'If Russia is really anti-Bolshevik, then a supply of equipment would enable it to redeem itself. If Russia is pro-Bolshevik, not merely is it none of our business to interfere with its internal affairs, it would be positively mischievous: it would strengthen and consolidate Bolshevik opinion ... We cannot afford the burden ... if we are committed to a war against a continent like Russia, it is

> 'Winston is in Paris. He wants to conduct a war against the Bolsheviks. That would cause a revolution! Our people would not permit it.'
>
> LLOYD GEORGE

the road to bankruptcy and Bolshevism in these islands.'[27] Lloyd George experienced considerable difficulty in reining Churchill in.

Nevertheless, Britain did intervene, albeit on a relatively small scale. According to Lloyd George, British support of the White forces cost some £100 million and 329 British lives. For many months Churchill had much faith in General Anton Denikin, an ardent supporter of the Russian Empire, who led southern White Russians for two years from April 1918. Churchill, nevertheless, had to warn Denikin that British financial backing would end if he did not stop the anti-Jewish atrocities committed by his forces. Churchill day-dreamed that when Denikin took Moscow he, Churchill, would be the real architect of a democratic constitution for Russia. Again Churchill's over-zealous championing of his cause harmed him politically. Even Arthur Balfour, who was himself hostile to the Bolsheviks, was moved to comment after a Cabinet meeting in which Churchill argued for Denikin, 'I admire the exaggerated way you tell the truth'. Some of the British press took to referring to the campaign as 'Mr Churchill's Private War'.

Churchill also took a robust line on the increasing violence in Ireland after the end of the war. The British military campaign in Ireland was the responsibility of the Chief Secretary for Ireland, but Churchill was responsible for providing the necessary troops. Faced with demands for troops at home, India, Egypt and elsewhere, Churchill successfully urged that a special force of 8,000 former soldiers be raised. In due course, these men, who wore a mixture of army and Royal Irish Constabulary uniforms, became known as the 'Black and Tans' and were notorious for violent reprisals in nationalist areas of Ireland. Churchill, like Lloyd George, was very willing to take responsibility for reprisals, both recognising that this increased the likelihood that they would be targets for assassination. From November 1920 Churchill was assigned a personal bodyguard by Scotland Yard, for many years Detective Sergeant Walter H Thompson.

Churchill saw Irish terrorism as part of a *world-wide conspiracy against our country* which was *designed to deprive us of our place in the world and rob us of victory*.[28] Churchill often believed Bolshevism and nationalism were intertwined, and this was especially so in Egypt after the First World War where railway strikes accompanied nationalist unrest. While strongly supporting continued British rule in India, Churchill was outraged by General Reginald Dyer's massacre of 379 unarmed Indian people (with over 1,200 wounded) at Amritsar in 1919. In July 1920 Churchill gave one of his finest speeches in which he defended the government and criticised Dyer, contrasting *the lawful authority* of the British Empire and *the British way of doing business* with Dyer's policy of shoot-to-kill until ammunition ran low, while repeating his detestation of *the world-wide character of the seditious and revolutionary movement with which we are confronted*.[29]

Churchill served also as Secretary of State for Air while at the War Office from 1919 to 1921. He had been an advocate of the military value of aircraft since January 1909 and he sent a message of support to the first meeting of the Aerial League of the British Empire that April. At the Admiralty he had founded the Royal Naval Air Service. He had also begun to learn to fly in 1912 or 1913, stopping in 1914 but resuming in 1919. This ended with a serious crash at Croydon airport on 18 July 1919. His flying experiences provided copy for two articles in 1924. As Secretary of State Churchill was unsuccessful in securing Treasury money (at a time of severe public expenditure cuts, 'the Geddes axe') to maintain key civil aviation routes for the Empire.

He was more interested in military aviation, which he saw as the key to cheap but effective defence of the Empire. The RAF used air power effectively in Somaliland in 1919–20. Churchill made Sir Hugh Trenchard chief of the air staff and set him to work producing a scheme whereby Mesopotamia could be controlled by aircraft, armoured cars and fortified bases. At a major conference in Cairo in March 1921 Churchill and Trenchard put forward their plans which would substantially reduce the size of the army in the area and save millions of pounds yet maintain British control.

By this time Lloyd George had moved Churchill to the Colonial Office (from 13 February 1921). Churchill had successfully argued that the Colonial Office should be in charge of Britain's post-war Middle Eastern responsibilities, instead of the India Office controlling Iraq and the Foreign Office Palestine. He continued actively to pursue British Middle Eastern interests while at the Colonial Office. In March 1921 he visited Jerusalem and in the face of Arab protests restated British intentions to establish a Jewish National Home in Palestine, but he also ended Zionist hopes of Jewish settlements spreading east of the Jordan. His period as Secretary of State for the Colonies was also notable for his interest in fostering East African economic development (thereby following up his 1908 travels) and for his restrictions on Indian immigrants to that area.

Churchill's career as a Liberal politician effectively ended with the fall of Lloyd George's Coalition government on 19 October 1922 when the majority of Conservative MPs withdrew their support at a meeting held at the Carlton Club. Churchill was in hospital, having been operated on for appendicitis the night before. He had only partially recovered when he went to Dundee for the closing stages of the general election campaign. He and his fellow National Liberal lost their seats to Edwin Scrymgeour, the local Prohibitionist and socialist, and E G Morel, the Labour candidate who had been a notable critic of British entry into the First World War.

Churchill had been the second most influential Liberal Coalitionist after Lloyd George. He had been a stalwart supporter of the Prime Minister on many issues, including during the Chanak crisis of September 1922, which for a while threatened to result in war between Britain and Turkey. Yet he had been drifting further away from most of his fellow Coalition Liberals and their radical social concerns and on some issues he was closer to the politics of his friend F E Smith or the Conservative Diehards. This was so in regard to Russia and to anti-socialism generally. It was also the case on India, General Dyer apart, and many other imperial issues. Yet it was not so in 1922 with regard to Free Trade, nor with Ireland, where Churchill's conciliatory contribution to a settlement in late 1921, was contrary to Tory backbench sentiments. On top of such policy differences, many Conservatives loathed Churchill for changing party and, in their eyes, for being given to reckless and brash adventures. In late 1922 his political career appeared to be in terminal decline.

Chapter 3: In Defence of the British Empire and the Constitution, 1922–40

Churchill renewed his career twice between 1922 and 1940. Like a cat, he seemed to have several lives. He politically realigned himself in the early 1920s and from 1924–9 followed in his father's footsteps in being Chancellor of the Exchequer. Having fallen out of step again with the Conservative Party in the early to mid-1930s, his political opportunity came with the outbreak of a major war in Europe in 1939. He returned to the Admiralty at a Conservative Prime Minister's request.

In late 1922 Churchill could view the party political wreckage left after the premiership of Lloyd George (1916–22). The Liberal Party had been overtaken in the number of its parliamentary seats by the Labour Party and was split between followers of Asquith and Lloyd George. The Coalition Conservative leadership, including Austen Chamberlain, Arthur Balfour and F E Smith, had been disavowed by the bulk of the parliamentary party and appeared to be a floating body of talent similar to the followers of Sir Robert Peel after 1846. Earlier, Churchill had been a keen supporter of 'fusion', the merging of the Coalition Liberals and the Coalition Conservatives; a move from which he would have been the major beneficiary as the most prominent right-wing Coalition Liberal. With no such new centre-right bloc in being, Churchill had to look to a political future with the Conservative Party.

To his life-long theme of supporting and praising the British Empire, from 1917 he added, as a core political belief, anti-socialism. Paul Addison has written of his time as Secretary of State for War (1919–21), 'Churchill's Marlborough complex was coupled with a primal hatred of the Bolshevik revolution'.[1] His determined support for the White forces fighting in Russia combined with his belief that the Third International was an effective organiser of subversion in Britain and the British Empire made his credentials as an anti-Bolshevik and a defender of order unquestionable. To his Dundee opponent, Edwin Scrymgeour, Churchill was too much the anti-socialist Man of Action. During the 1922 general election campaign, which was held soon after Benito Mussolini took power in Italy, he observed that it would not surprise him in the event of civil war in Britain 'if Mr Churchill were at the head of the Fascisti party'.[2] This was to ignore Churchill's reverence for the British constitution and commitment to democracy, yet it reflected Churchill's belligerent stance during the 1910–26 era of serious industrial unrest and much use of class war rhetoric.

Even after Mussolini assumed dictatorial powers in 1925 and banned all other parties in 1926, Churchill could praise his anti-Communist policies. In 1927 he visited Italy with his son and his brother, and, as Chancellor of the Exchequer, saw the Italian minister of finance concerning war debts. He also briefly met Mussolini twice. He outraged both Liberals and Labour in Britain by saying that if he had been Italian he would have been with Mussolini in the struggle against *the bestial appetites and passions of Leninism*. Given Mussolini's imprisonment of trade unionists and socialists as well as communists, this strengthened hostility to Churchill on the Left in Britain. Such hostility was not assuaged by Churchill's later elaboration that Mussolini's methods were inappropriate in a long-established parliamentary democracy such as Britain. Yet Churchill's main concern was the security of Britain and the British Empire. He had been outraged when Mussolini had occupied Fiume, disregarding the League of Nations. He commented to Clementine, *What a swine this Mussolini is.*[3] He was similarly angered in the mid-1930s by Mussolini's invasion of Abyssinia. While rightly recognising Hitler as the major threat to Britain, he continued to have hopes of Mussolini siding with Britain in the Mediterranean and as late as October 1937 publicly praised his anti-communist role in Italy. While Churchill had outstanding anti-socialist credentials, he also could appeal to Conservative Empire loyalists by his unquestionable commitment to the British Empire. To a considerable extent his view of the Empire was frozen in 1896–1908, the period of his military exploits and travels.

Churchill's commitment to Free Trade became weaker during the 1920s. In the 1923 general election, called by Stanley Baldwin on the issue of protection, Churchill was still unequivocal as to his faith in Free Trade. He issued a press statement on 11 November 1923.

… an aggressive attack has been levelled needlessly and wantonly at the foundations of the people's livelihood. A monstrous fallacy is erected against us. Nearly all the trades of the country are threatened with injury.

He stood for Leicester West as a Liberal Free Trader, but lost to Labour. In attacking Labour, he proclaimed his belief in individualism: *Socialism considers primarily the man, whereas Liberalism seeks to elevate the individual. Socialism exalts the* conception of the State; Liberalism cherishes the ideal of the home. Socialism aims at reducing the whole of the citizens to a uniform level, and keeping them when so reduced at that level. Liberalism aims at building up a minimum standard of life and raising it gradually, year by year as the general growth of wealth renders it possible.[4] When Liberal support put Labour into office for the first time in January 1924, Churchill was outraged. In a letter to the *Times* on 18 January he commented, *The enthronement in office of a socialist government will be a serious national misfortune such as has usually befallen great States only on the morrow of defeat in war*. His letter marked his break with the Liberal Party and, in effect, the issue of anti-socialism outweighing other issues.

The enthronement in office of a socialist government will be a serious national misfortune such as has usually befallen great States only on the morrow of defeat in war.

CHURCHILL

Churchill was a powerful political cannon, even if often a loose one; and if he did not explode in his own side's face, he was a valuable force. He was still under 50 in early 1924. For the Conservatives he also represented one of the leading discontented Liberals whose anti-Labour beliefs might bring both MPs and a greater body of electors to the Conservative camp. Baldwin and other leading Conservatives were very willing to set aside past feelings about Churchill if he delivered them power, in the way that the Liberal Unionists had buttressed Conservative hegemony in politics from 1886–1905. Given his robust Liberal stance in November–December 1923 Clementine Churchill and Churchill's genuine friends feared that he might discredit himself by moving too fast back to the Conservatives.

In March 1924 he stood in the Westminster Abbey by-election. His way was eased by the local Conservatives pointing out that their Association was entitled 'constitutional' not 'Conservative'. It was harmed by the Association, in spite of its leaders, adopting the nephew of the previous MP. At his adoption meeting Churchill declared, *I am an Independent Anti-Socialist candidate* and *I am not in the least deceived by the moderation of the present Socialist government.* He warned that they were socialists in wait for a Parliamentary majority and on winning one would return to the doctrines of *the nationalisation of all the means of production, distribution and exchange.* He linked his condemnation of *This vast Socialist scheme of State slavery* with an appeal of a very old-fashioned kind *to our administrators in the great Oriental countries – to India and Egypt – to inspire them with confidence in their work and give them the feeling that the old country has not lost heart or faith in its destiny and its mission of right and justice throughout the world and that if they do their duty faithfully they will be supported and sustained.*[5] Here, his was the imperial voice of *noblesse oblige.* Although more than 20 Conservative MPs had come out openly in favour of Churchill, he still lost, although by only 43 votes.

By July 1924 the Conservative leadership had agreed to Churchill being supported in a safe Conservative seat as a 'Constitutionalist' candidate. In September he accepted nomination for Epping, just before the 1924 general election campaign. In his campaign he declared, *I represent uncompromising opposition to the subversive movement of Socialism, and I equally oppose those who are willing to make … compromising bargains with the Socialists.* He summarised his other campaign themes: *I am in favour of developing trade within the Empire, but I am not in favour of risking our money on Russia and other foreigners.*[6] He won with a majority of 9,763, securing a seat for life. His constituency was an hour and 20 minutes drive (via the Blackwall Tunnel) from Chartwell, near Westerham in Kent, his home from late 1922. He paid for Chartwell and subsequent major work on the house partly with money from selling the Londonderry Arms Hotel, Carnlough, on the Antrim coast, a property he had inherited in 1921 when Lord Henry Vane-Tempest, his cousin, had been killed in a train crash. He also used his earnings from *The World Crisis*, published in five books (six volumes) between 1923 and 1931.

He wrote much of *The World Crisis* while holding office under Lloyd George and Baldwin. The first volume was strengthened by Churchill's considerable knowledge of naval matters and that, following the attacks on him by Lord Esher in his *The Tragedy of Lord Kitchener*, 1921, he was allowed to defend himself by drawing on the official documents in his possession. Churchill, as Michael Wolff has commented, hoarded documents 'with the assiduity of a squirrel'. In his prefaces to the early volumes he liked to suggest that as his account was built on contemporary sources it was reliable. Later historians have been critical of his account, not least of its disproportionate attention to Gallipoli. Robin Prior, in an analysis of the volumes dealing with 1911–18, has pointed to Churchill's frequent reference to 'the fates' which he commented Churchill used 'not to explain events but to explain them away'. Nevertheless, Prior and others have praised the volumes for their analysis of casualty statistics, the account of the Battle of the Somme, their style and for the 'thread of humanity' which runs through these substantial books.[7]

The 1924 general election saw the defeat of the first Labour government, the ending of the Liberal Party as a potential part of government and a major victory for the Conservative Party. It brought Baldwin back to the premiership after his disastrous throwing away of a Conservative majority after only a year in a bid to get the electorate's backing for protection. In the 1923 general election Churchill had had much fun with Baldwin's U-turn on trade policy, recalling ... *his first act* [as Prime Minister] *was to send for Mr McKenna and to ask this eminent Free Trade financial authority to be his righthand man as Chancellor of the Exchequer. All through the summer Mr Baldwin has been beseeching Mr McKenna to come to his aid. Right down to August he was still urging Mr McKenna to join him.* He also enjoyed ridiculing Baldwin. For instance: *Mr Baldwin, our Prime Minister, is a very honest man.* (Laughter.) *I for one could have been ready to believe that, even if he had not told us so often.* (Laughter.) *It is a fine thing to be honest, but it is also very important for a Prime Minister to be right.*[8]

A year after Baldwin had been the butt of Churchill's wit, he offered him Lord Randolph's old post, Chancellor of the Exchequer. Baldwin and his associates saw Churchill as a probable asset in government but a certain danger if left to lead dissident backbenchers or alternatively former members of Lloyd George's coalition government. Already, after the election, Churchill had been acclaimed as the pre-eminent anti-socialist at a dinner in his honour given at the Constitutional Club by a group of right-wing Conservatives. The historian Stuart Ball has suggested that Churchill was too right-wing by this time and Baldwin put him where he could do little harm.[9] Perhaps, more likely, he was both keeping him under some control and using him as the new McKenna, a clear sign that it was not to be a protectionist government.

Churchill took over his father's post after a 38-year interval, on 6 November 1924 and held the post until 4 June 1929. He wore his father's old robes of office, which his mother had kept. In accepting the post, he told Baldwin, *This fulfils my ambition*, although it was not an area of his expertise or of particular interest to him. He did not bring innovative ideas to the post, instead behaving in a steady and reliable manner, presenting consensus economic policies in his own vivid language. His father had destroyed his career by insisting on Gladstonian economy in state finance. In a more prudent manner, but with great determination, Churchill held down levels of public expenditure, including for the navy, and reduced the level of income tax. In seeking to keep defence expenditure down, Churchill supported financial planning where it was presumed that for the next ten-year period there would be no war, until such time as there was a serious threat. This Ten Year Rule became controversial in the 1930s. The appeasers could argue that he was responsible for rearmament starting from a low level, while Churchill could counter that Hitler's coming to power in 1933 marked the kind of threat which was always intended to end the ten-year policy.

The other major controversy of his Chancellorship was the decision to return to the Gold Standard at the pre-First World War parity with the dollar. The economist John Maynard Keynes and the former Chancellor and banker Reginald McKenna debated the issue with Treasury experts and Churchill, but Churchill went for orthodoxy and the easier political option. Keynes castigated this decision in his book, *The Economic Consequences of Mr Churchill* (1925), a sequel (at least in its title) to his *The Economic Consequences of the Peace* (1919). To go back to the Gold Standard made much sense for Britain as it was the country which exported a higher proportion of its manufacturing output than any other and was also a very major exporter of capital. Hence Britain had a major interest in international currency stability. However, the problem was that while other currencies went back on to the Gold Standard at different rates, to reflect their changed relative strengths after the war, Britain's return may have overvalued the pound by up to 10 per cent (Keynes' estimate), with very bad results for British exports.

At the time Churchill was praised for making a hard decision. Within two years he was having doubts.

Churchill also distinguished himself as a hawk in the General Strike and the six-month long coal dispute of 1926. He saw the General Strike as a constitutional challenge: *if it is fought out to a conclusion, can only end in the overthrow of Parliamentary government or in its decisive victory*. He argued that in the event of a victory for the TUC *the existing constitution will be fatally injured, and ...* [events] *will inevitably lead to the erection of some Soviet of trade unions on which ... the real effective control of the economic and political life of the country will devolve.*[10] During the General Strike he appeared to be one of the ministers least desirous of a negotiated settlement to the mining dispute. Baldwin, fearing Churchill's probable belligerence in other roles, put him in charge of producing a government newssheet, *The British Gazette*. Using volunteer labour, Churchill edited eight issues which by the last two issues had print runs of some two million copies. Churchill's excesses as editor were often curbed by J C C Davidson, the Parliamentary Secretary at the Admiralty and a close associate of Baldwin. Davidson wrote of Churchill's militaristic outlook on the government's Supply and Transport Committee when a convoy was to be sent to the docks: 'Winston was all for a tremendous display of force; machine guns, hidden but there, should be placed along the route; tanks should be used in addition to armoured cars; and so on.'[11]

'Winston was all for a tremendous display of force; machine guns, hidden but there, should be placed along the route; tanks should be used in addition to armoured cars; and so on.'

J C C DAVIDSON

Once the General Strike was called off, he took a more magnanimous view of the miners' dispute, deeming it a legitimate industrial struggle and advocating a moderate settlement. Arthur Steel-Maitland wrote of his ability as a speaker but regretted his attempts to bully the miners. He commented, 'He's jolly difficult when he's in a napoleon-esque attitude, dictating instructions in military metaphors, and the spotlight full on him.'[12] However, when Churchill's efforts failed, he took a tough line again, being willing to restrict welfare help to miners and their families in order to force a speedier end to the dispute. Churchill's image as a person who delighted in defying organised labour did him much harm with some sections of the working class until 1940.

In the 1929 general election Baldwin appealed to the country on the theme of 'Safety First'. Churchill, building on his tight financial policies as Chancellor of the Exchequer, spoke repeatedly on the theme of the Socialist's *policy of pillage and plunder* and Lloyd George's *policy of squander*. His second theme was that both Labour and the Liberals would seriously damage the Empire, whereas he could conjure up a vision in which, under the Conservatives, *the British Empire and the United States could walk forward side by side, leading mankind in majesty and peace.*

The Conservatives lost the general election and Labour formed a second minority government. Although Churchill's term as Chancellor of the Exchequer was not innovative, he was deemed to have been sound. While Neville Chamberlain had been positioning himself to be Baldwin's crown prince, much as Lloyd George had under Asquith, Churchill and Sir Douglas Hogg (the Attorney General and then Lord Chancellor as Lord Hailsham) were the other names mentioned in the later 1920s. However, Churchill put himself out of the running not only to be leader but even to be given office by his Die Hard stance on India. Much of the Conservative Party had been outraged by the Irish settlement of 1921–2. For those committed to the British Empire the policy of Ramsay MacDonald's Labour government and of Lord Irwin (later Viscount Halifax) to move India towards Dominion status was anathema. Baldwin had made clear his support for such a policy in October 1929 when Churchill was in New York.

Churchill, who had shown some degree of sensitivity to Islam when writing of the wars with the Dervishes, was notably disparaging of Hinduism. He commented in the *Daily Mail* on 16 November 1925, *The rescue of India from ages of barbarism, tyranny and internecine war* had been hindered by the British *forbearance we promised to observe towards Indian religious and social customs*. Churchill was indignant when Sir John Reith, the Managing Director of the BBC, would not accept his offer of paying the BBC £100 to make a ten-minute broadcast on the subject of India.[13] Churchill spoke out against Gandhi and the nationalists, saying that they would have to be crushed.

On 28 January 1931 he resigned from the Opposition Business Committee and retired to the backbenches for the subsequent eight and a half years. He continued to be outspoken, stating at an Indian Empire Society meeting in the Free Trade Hall, Manchester, on 30 January 1931, that Britain should make it *perfectly clear that we intend to remain the effective rulers of India in every essential for a very long and indefinite period, and that though we welcome co-operation in every branch of government from loyal and faithful Indians, we will have no truck with lawlessness or treason and will, if necessary, suspend even the most modest constitutional change* ... He concluded: *The loss of India ... would be final and fatal to us. It could not fail to be part of a process which would reduce us to the scale of a minor Power ... We have forty-five millions in this island, a very large proportion of whom are in existence because of our world position, economic, political, imperial.*[14]

India was not the only divisive issue for the Conservatives. There were also conflicts within the party over Lord Beaverbrook's Empire Free Trade crusade. Beaverbrook was an old friend of Churchill and even tried to convert him to his cause. According to Harold Nicolson, who was present at a dinner party given by Beaverbrook, 'Winston says that he has abandoned all his convictions and clings to the conviction of free trade as the only one which is left to him.' Churchill's parting of the ways with the other Conservative leaders actually began, as in 1903–4, with tariffs. When Baldwin pledged himself to tariffs at the next election on 14 October 1930, Churchill saw Baldwin to tell him he dissented but made no public protest. Churchill changed his views with the world economic crisis, announcing his conversion to protection in a speech in his constituency on 11 September 1931.

Churchill's political isolation in the 1930s gave him further time and reason to write and to earn money by lecturing. His expensive lifestyle, not least living in and modifying Chartwell, had made writing an imperative in the 1920s, not least in 1922–4, the two years he was out of Parliament. While his major output in the 1920s was *The World Crisis*, he wrote many articles for *Cosmopolitan, Pall Mall* and *Strand* magazines, many of which he recycled in *Thoughts And Adventures* (1932), while a series of biographical essays published in these magazines and the *Daily Mail, News of the World* and *Sunday Pictorial* reappeared in *Great Contemporaries* (1937).

His major work published in the 1930s was *Marlborough: His Life and Times*, six volumes published between 1933 and 1938, which grew from a planned 200,000 words to over one million. He had wanted to write on Marlborough since the time he had completed his father's biography. Although written in large part to vindicate his ancestor from the accusations made by Macaulay, it rose above such partiality in its style and detailed research. Again it displayed Churchill's immense skill in writing gripping military history. The theme of the Grand Alliance in *Marlborough* was seen as topical by President Franklin Delano Roosevelt who, in the first of his letters in their lengthy Second World War correspondence, wrote on 11 September 1939, 'I am glad you did the Marlboro volumes before this thing started – and I much enjoyed reading them.'[15]

He also had more time to enjoy Chartwell and to paint. He had taken up painting after leaving the Admiralty in 1915, attracted to it when watching his sister-in-law 'Goonie' (Lady Gwendeline) Churchill painting in watercolours. He was further encouraged by the talented artists Hazel and John Lavery, and, later, Walter Sickert. Mary Soames, writing of her father, has estimated that of his surviving 500-plus paintings, about half date from 1930–9 which she has commented was 'a period when arguably Winston reached the peak of his powers as a painter'.[16]

Churchill lost some £10,000, then a huge sum, in the 1929 New York stock market crash. He was in New York on 'Black Thursday' and visited the gallery of the Wall Street stock exchange the next day. It was his some 30 years since he had previously been to the United States and Canada, then when lecturing after his Boer War exploits. In order to recoup his financial losses Churchill returned to the United States in December 1931 to give 40 lectures (for £10,000, with a further £7,000–8,000 for articles in the *Daily Mail*). Churchill's plans came unstuck when he was knocked down and seriously injured by a car in New York on 13 December. As a result he gave fewer lectures but still earned over £7,500. He went on to Toronto to deliver a further lecture (for an even higher fee for an individual lecture).[17]

As early as October 1930, before Hitler came to power,

Churchill expressed his belief that he had aggressive intentions towards France. When Churchill and his family visited Munich in summer 1932, Hitler had the opportunity to meet them but declined. They never did meet. From at least 1932 Churchill was concerned about Hitler's anti-Semitism. He condemned this and warned against German rearmament in the House of Commons in April 1933. Churchill saw Hitler as a menace to peace and a danger to the British Empire. In turn Hitler rightly judged Churchill to be one of his most implacable opponents in Britain.

While it would be wrong to suggest that Churchill was consistently hostile to appeasement, he was so most of the time. His deep distrust of Hitler helped keep him out of government. He was increasingly concerned as to British preparedness for a major European war, making the first of several major speeches on the need to improve Britain's air defences in the House of Commons in November 1934. Baldwin was more willing to listen to Churchill than was his successor as Prime Minister, Neville Chamberlain, though they both deemed Churchill to be lacking in judgement. After Churchill had again pressed for an urgent aircraft-building programme Baldwin involved both Churchill and his associate, Professor Frederick Lindemann, in government committees dealing with air defence.

However, Churchill threw away much of his accruing support by his ultra-royalist stance during the 1936 abdication crisis. What some interpreted as self-serving actions intended to undermine Baldwin were almost certainly symptoms of Churchill's romantic and archaic deference to the monarch. In July 1936 he had given the King's legal adviser, Walter Monckton, good advice. This was that Mrs Wallis Simpson should not seek a divorce from her second husband. When this was ignored, he hoped Beaverbrook would be successful in his attempt to get Wallis Simpson to withdraw her petition for divorce before it was made absolute, which would have defused the crisis. On 3 December Baldwin granted Edward VIII permission to consult Churchill, 'an old friend with whom he could talk freely'. Their discussion took place the next day, with Churchill feeling that the King should *have full time for his decision* and believing that matters could be postponed until the divorce was made absolute in April 1937. Churchill failed to grasp that the King was set on marriage and had no interest in postponing the announcement of the decision he had already made. As a result, Churchill's attempt to plead for time for the King and to justify his own actions during Question Time in the House of Commons on 7 December was a monumental misreading of the mood of the House. He was howled down. His young associate Robert Boothby estimated only seven MPs supported Churchill on that occasion. Churchill was devastated to see two years' work in recovering his position in politics undone. He remained a friend of the Duke and Duchess of Windsor after the abdication on 10 December 1936.

In spite of Churchill's forebodings at the time of the abdication, his reputation did bounce back as he became a focal point for those urging rearmament. Several people in the services and in the Civil Service risked their livelihoods to keep Churchill informed. Prominent among these were Desmond Morton, head of the Committee of Imperial Defence's Intelligence Centre, Ralph Wigram, head of the Central Department of the Foreign Office, Reginald Leeper, a senior Foreign Office official, Wing Commander Torr Anderson and Sir Robert Vansittart, the Permanent Under-Secretary of State for Foreign Affairs, 1930–8. Churchill's political experience and charisma attracted to him a group of younger Conservative MPs, notably Brendan Bracken, Robert Boothby and Duncan Sandys, his son-in-law. There was initially a separate group, including Harold Macmillan, Duff Cooper, Leo Amery, Ronald Cartland, Ronald Tree, J P L Thomas and Lord Cranborne (later Salisbury) around Anthony Eden, Foreign Secretary 1935–8. The Churchill and Eden groups increasingly came together after the German occupation of Czechoslovakia.

Churchill earlier had been optimistic for a while that Czechoslovakia could be maintained yet the Sudeten Germans satisfied with a scheme of local autonomy. He and Lindemann were unduly impressed when, in May 1938, they met Conrad Henlein, the Sudeten German leader through the auspices of Vansittart. However, he was soon disillusioned. He condemned Chamberlain's Munich agreement as *a total and unmitigated defeat*.[18] Chamberlain's supporters, including in Churchill's constituency, denounced him and Chamberlain rebuffed Churchill's desire to join the government in order to organise rapid rearmament. As the historian R A C Parker wrote of Churchill and Chamberlain, 'Both intended to preserve the independence of Britain and its Empire. Their methods were totally different.'[19]

In the Norway debate of 1940, Chamberlain's majority in the Commons was reduced to only 81 votes, with 33 government supporters voting with the Opposition and over 60 abstentions. However, some of these Conservative MPs had sought only to signal to the government that it should be formed on a wider, more 'national' basis to better run the war, not to displace Chamberlain. Both Chamberlain and the King favoured the Foreign Secretary, Lord Halifax, as his successor, but he declined to push hard for the post, and Churchill secured the premiership. Chamberlain retained the leadership of the Conservative Party and considerable support in Parliament, and was consequently treated with great respect by Churchill.

With the German invasion of Poland, any desire for negotiating with Hitler ended for nearly all British politicians. With the outbreak of war on 3 September 1939, after a decade out of office and at the age of 64, Churchill returned to the Admiralty as First Lord and was also a member of the War Cabinet. The Fleet received the signal 'Winston is back' and Churchill took vigorous control, sending demands for action or for information in all directions. While seeking no new Gallipoli, Churchill nevertheless came up with ideas for utilising British naval strength. He considered 'forcing a passage into the Baltic', seizing Narvik, the port for Swedish iron ore exports to Germany, and mining Norwegian territorial waters. His period of office saw some major British losses, most notably the aircraft carrier *Courageous* in September and the *Royal Oak* at Scapa Flow in October 1939, but he could report some successes, ranging from action against the German pocket battleship *Graf Spee* in December 1939, the release of 299 Allied prisoners from the German supply ship *Altmark* in February 1940 and the sinking of several U-boats.

However, he was involved in a major failure of the first part of the war, the unsuccessful attempts to assist Norway. The Navy neither blocked nor impeded the German invasion of that country and Churchill did not fully benefit from the new intelligence information from Enigma ciphers. The failures were offset to a limited extent by the destruction of ten German destroyers in Narvik Fjord and, in late April 1940, by the successful evacuation of troops from central Norway. Although Churchill loyally supported Neville Chamberlain over Norway, the issue brought Chamberlain down and Churchill to the premiership on 10 May 1940.

Part Two

THE LEADERSHIP

Chapter 4: The British Empire Alone, 1940–1

Churchill, who had been a thrusting young minister of 31 in 1905, finally reached the top of the greasy pole (Disraeli's phrase) at the then usual retirement age of 65. This was later than William Gladstone, at the ages of 25 and 57, but sooner than Lord Palmerston, at the ages of 23 and 70, of other notable early-achieving premiers of the previous 100 years.

Churchill certainly had both broad ministerial experience and what Denis Healey dubbed 'a broad hinterland'. He had not been Foreign Secretary but nevertheless his ministerial experience was outstanding: Chancellor of the Exchequer, Home Secretary, Secretary of State for War, First Lord of the Admiralty, Secretary of State for Air, Minister of Munitions, Secretary of State for the Colonies, President of the Board of Trade and Chancellor of the Duchy of Lancaster. In addition he had had a short military career, involving combat experience in a series of imperial campaigns. He was undoubtedly a brave man, but one who had to mentally prepare himself to show no fear in battle or in civilian life. Walter Thompson, his personal detective, recalled him cringing with fear by a wall when a fast car narrowly missed him in the Bahamas shortly after his bad accident in New York in 1931. When Thompson said he needed to overcome such fears, Churchill responded, *It will not occur again*, and it did not.[1] Although obsessed with politics, he had other outlets as a journalist, author and painter. His powers of expression in his books had been good in *The Malakand Field Force* but had been outstanding thereafter. These powers of vivid expression played a major part in his leadership of the British people during the Second World War.

Like Lloyd George in the First World War, Churchill took over in the dark days of a major war and although not leader of a major party, headed a coalition government. In some ways Churchill could be seen as a one-man coalition. He combined both Conservative and Liberal political pasts. More than this, he was seen for many years as the embodiment (with his friend F E Smith) of over-clever Lloyd George coalitionism, the return of which concerned Baldwin for some years. Yet, in other respects he had appeared as something of a combination of part dinosaur of Victorian imperialism with the more chilling part of an inter-war right-wing Man of Action, as epitomised by D'Annunzio's seizure of Fiume and Mussolini's march on Rome. British Labour admired his anti-Nazi record, but remembered his record in the General Strike and the mining dispute in 1926 and his vigorous anti-socialist politics, as well as his erstwhile praise for Benito Mussolini and General Francisco Franco. Lord Halifax, the alternative successor to Neville Chamberlain, had at least been promoting Indian progress to Dominion status while Churchill had been digging a deeper last ditch in which to obstruct such change. Yet during the war Churchill was mindful that he headed a coalition. It was, for instance, a major reason why, when both he and Anthony Eden were about to depart from Yalta in early 1945, he advised the King that if both of them were killed to appoint in his place Sir John Anderson, emphasising that he was an Independent National Member of Parliament.

Churchill's experiences of the First World War had taught

him the hard way that to achieve the immortal fame that he craved, he needed not only to make history but to write it. He had seen that need with his evidence to the Dardanelles Inquiry and then *The World Crisis*. He had also vindicated his ancestor Duke John in his *Marlborough*, undoing, he hoped, the bitterly critical assessments of Macaulay. The care which went into his moulding of history and the extensiveness of these efforts to create his own far-sighted and principled role before and during the Second World War, based on much fact but more than a little additional myth, has been the subject of recent reassessments, notably by Sheila Lawlor and David Reynolds.[2] Churchill long pre-dated the 'spin doctors' of the 1990s and after. Having made a massive contribution to Britain's war effort, he added his own stamp of approval in six volumes with *The Second World War* (1948–54). His life had also prepared him for this task. He had immortalised his own exploits in a series of books and essays from *The Malakand Field Force* through *My Early Life* to the great histories of the two World Wars. Yet, none of this, separating Churchill's actions, hesitancies and mistakes included from the legend, undercuts the fundamental fact that he was an able and inspiring war leader, albeit one who made some major mistakes and showed anything but magnanimity to several people who crossed him or whom he deemed (sometimes unfairly) not up to their jobs. In recognising this, caution needs to be taken in writing of others lest the sole benchmark for assessing their contributions to the waging of the Second World War is whether or not Churchill approved of them.

Churchill's experience of government in the First World War, supplemented by that of civil servants and his friend Beaverbrook, who held high office in both wars, contributed to Churchill's highly personal style of running his wartime administration. However, much of the machinery of wartime administration was in place under Neville Chamberlain. Lord Hankey described it in 1945, 'The new War Cabinet ... was based on Mr Lloyd George's system brought up to date ... by the establishment of the Chiefs of Staff Committee and the Joint Planning and Joint Intelligence organisations behind it'. As Churchill told the House of Commons, *I do not, of course, conduct this war from day to day myself; it is conducted from day to day, and in its future outlook by the Chiefs of Staff Committee.* In 1941 he presided at only 44 of 462 meetings of this committee. He also told the Commons that he worked *under the supervision and control of the War Cabinet*, whose agreement he needed on all major decisions. He did, however, defend his changes in the machinery of government. He commented, *It is now the fashion to speak of the Lloyd George War Cabinet as if it gave universal satisfactions and conducted the war with unerring judgement and unbroken success. On the contrary, complaints were loud and clamant.* He made it clear that he would not be *living up slavishly to the standards and methods of the past.* [3]

While Churchill was ready to adapt the machinery of government to his needs, he brought to 10 Downing Street his near-hyperactivity which, while it had some negative results was generally valuable in energising higher government. Edward Bridges, the secretary to the War Cabinet, later commented that 'within a few days of his becoming Prime Minister, the whole machinery of government was working at a pace, and with an intensity of purpose, quite unlike anything which had gone before ... His experience of Government business enabled him to pick out the points on which prompt decisions were needed ...

'Within a few days of {Churchill} becoming Prime Minister, the whole machinery of government was working at a pace, and with an intensity of purpose, quite unlike anything which had gone before ...'

EDWARD BRIDGES

'. He also imparted his sense of urgency – and indicated the recipient's responsibility in the rapid carrying-out of business – with his 'Action This Day' slips on many minutes.[4] In transmitting urgency and energy he was supreme but not unique, Beaverbrook and Field Marshal Montgomery being among the few with such abilities.

Churchill liked to surround himself with a circle of people whom he respected and trusted. These needed to be professionals in their jobs. But more than this, they needed to be loyal to Churchill, to work towards his aims and, preferably, only to argue if thereby they were helping to achieve his ends. Where those working for him were faced with the need for unexpected decisions, he expected that his close circle would know what he would want done. In a way this was a much milder version of what Sir Ian Kershaw has dubbed 'working towards the *Führer*' in his biography of Hitler. Churchill's was a heavily paternalistic leadership. Perhaps it had elements of him being the leader of his gang (like a schoolboy). He also displayed a continuing taste for medals, paying for a set of them for the War Cabinet members and selected others. His very own campaign medals read, 'THE GREAT COALITION 1940–1945'. Those who matched up to his expectations basked in the warmth of his friendship. Sir Leslie Rowan, his Private Secretary 1941–5, recalled his pleasure that Churchill had shown him 'such friendship and trust', adding 'None of us would ever betray that trust.' For those who served Churchill well, his friendship was also shown in considerable kindness and generosity. One notable example, from before the war, was when the daughter of his police bodyguard appeared doomed to deafness, Churchill had her seen by a Harley Street specialist and paid the bills for the ensuing successful operation.[5] However, with those who failed to match up to Churchill's requirements, he could be stern, even brutal. He had few, if any, compunctions, in dismissing subordinates. In 1941 he ended the civil service career of Frank Pick, the former deputy head of London Transport, when he refused to present aircraft loss statistics in an unduly favourable way as Churchill wished. Churchill was also ready to dispense with major figures, even when, as in the case of General Sir Claude Auchinleck, he liked them.

Soon after taking office, Churchill had to show decisiveness and to take brutal decisions. This was especially so with the fall of France. At immense personal risk he repeatedly flew to France to meet with the leading ministers and generals to encourage them to fight on. He took up the suggestion of Jean Monnet, backed by Charles de Gaulle, that the French will to fight on would be strengthened by *proclaiming the indissoluble union of our two peoples and of our two Empires* and secured the War Cabinet's support.[6] With the ending of French resistance Churchill argued in the War Cabinet that the release of the French government from the agreement that neither country should enter into separate negotiations should be subject to *an absolute condition ... that the French Fleet should sail forthwith for British ports pending any discussion of armistice terms.*[7] After Marshal Pétain's government had signed an armistice the French were obliged to prevent their fleet falling into British hands. Churchill readily agreed with A V Alexander, First Lord of the Admiralty, Sir Dudley Pound, Chief of the Naval Staff, and Lord Beaverbrook that it was essential to destroy the French fleet at Oran if it would not surrender to the British. On 3 July 1940 in the space of nine minutes nearly all the French fleet was destroyed, with 1,250 French sailors killed. This ruthless action convinced American, Russian and other leaders that Britain was determined to fight Nazi Germany.

Churchill had expressed some private concern at the task which he was taking on when he had become premier. He then commented to his bodyguard, *God alone knows how great it is. I hope that it is not too late. I am very much afraid that it is. We can only do our best.* In public then and later he displayed resolute determination to lead a fight to the finish. This was so even with the fall of France. As Sheila Lawlor has commented, 'Whereas amongst his colleagues (both politicians and professionals) there was a sense of doom and horror at what seemed to be the hopelessness of Britain in face of the inevitable unfolding of events, Churchill seemed more quickly to recover buoyancy.'[8]

Churchill's indomitableness came from his taste for war, as displayed in 1896–1900, his faith in his destiny, his understanding of British history and his hopes of powerful help from 'the English speaking peoples', both in British Empire and the United States. Churchill once commented, *the longer you can look back, the further you can look forward.*[9] He could draw on his considerable government experience in both war and peace but also his understanding of British history. For his own stirring speeches Churchill drew inspiration from Queen Elizabeth I's speech at Tilbury in 1588, when Spanish invasions seemed imminent. She boosted the morale of her troops with her resolve 'to live or die amongst you all, to lay down ... my honour and my blood even in the dust'. These were words which Churchill reprinted in the second volume of *A History Of The English Speaking Peoples*, published in 1956 but drafted before the war. After the successful evacuation of British and allied troops from Dunkirk, Churchill

> *We shall fight on the beaches, we shall fight on the landing grounds, we shall fight in the fields and streets, we shall fight in the hills; we shall never surrender.*
>
> CHURCHILL

reported to the House of Commons on 4 June 1940, making his famous peroration which included, *We shall fight on the beaches, we shall fight on the landing grounds, we shall fight in the fields and streets, we shall fight in the hills; we shall never surrender*, and ended with the claim that if the very worst happened, *our Empire beyond the seas ... would carry on the struggle, until, in God's good time, the new world, with all its power and might, steps forth to the rescue and liberation of the old.*[10]

Churchill exhibited much personal bravery, even recklessness, during the Battle of Britain, from July to October 1940, and the Blitz. He visited Fighter Command at Stanmore three times in August and September and anti-aircraft battery personnel, including his daughter Mary, sometimes when air raids were in progress. In the Blitz he was dilatory in going to deep air-raid shelters and often watched German bombing from the roof top of the Annexe to 10 Downing Street. Churchill held the widespread fatalism of the period, once observing during an air raid, *When my time is due, it will come.* He also had confidence in his sense of destiny, telling his bodyguard not to fuss: *I have a mission to perform and That Person will see that it is performed.*[11] In this link to God, there are echoes of Gladstone's frequent justifications of his political actions.

Churchill was more usually concerned with his links with Roosevelt than with God. Churchill quickly replaced his head of British secret intelligence in the United States with William Stephenson, a Canadian who had been involved in a failed attempt by Churchill in early 1940 to sabotage Swedish supplies of iron ore to Germany. British intelligence in London (MI5) foiled a plot by Tyler Kent, a US cipher clerk, to provide Roosevelt's political opponents in the US with some 1,500 documents from the US Embassy in London. This led to Churchill having British fascists and fascist sympathisers rounded up and interned. After Roosevelt's special envoy William Donovan, a wealthy New York lawyer, visited

Franklin Roosevelt

Britain depended on support from major allies for victory in the Second World War. These were the superpowers, the United States and the Soviet Union. The Anglo-American alliance was economically and militarily vital – and became more so as the war went on. The crucial person for Churchill was Franklin Delano Roosevelt, the president of the United States since 1933 and the American wartime leader until his death on 12 April 1945. Roosevelt was born at Hyde Park, New York, on 30 January 1882, the only son of James and Sara Delano Roosevelt. After studying at Harvard and Columbia Universities, he became a lawyer. He was elected to the New York State Senate in 1910 and held office under President Woodrow Wilson (1913–21). He was seriously disabled by poliomyelitis from 1921. Nevertheless, he recovered sufficiently to be elected governor of New York State, 1929–32, and then President of the United States. During the 1930s Roosevelt responded to the world recession with the New Deal.

Roosevelt and Churchill first met in London in 1918 when Roosevelt was Assistant Secretary to the Navy. They next met at Placentia Bay in August 1941. They worked well together, with mutual respect and a personal friendship (though this was warmer with Churchill). Churchill, prone to emotion, was in tears at Roosevelt's memorial service in London on 17 April 1945. In the House of Commons his tribute to Roosevelt included the statement that Roosevelt had been 'the greatest American friend we have ever known'. However, while united in their determination to beat Germany and Japan, they were both mindful of their own countries' priorities. Roosevelt had no intention of restoring the British Empire or maintaining British naval supremacy. He pressed for democracy, free markets and the free movement of capital. He was also a realist in terms of power, recognising the bargaining power of the Soviet Union after the Red Army had pushed the German forces back from Stalingrad into Germany and the weakening position of Britain in the latter stages of the war. Nevertheless, the good relations between Roosevelt and Churchill played a major role in Anglo-American co-operation 1941–5.

London and reported favourably on British determination to withstand an invasion, Roosevelt went ahead with a considerable degree of collaboration with Britain, including in intelligence matters and the releasing of 50 surplus destroyers in exchange for leases on British air and naval bases of strategic importance to the United States.[12]

While the British Empire was isolated, Churchill was especially keen to help the Free French cause. After Oran, Charles de Gaulle made a broadcast to France, expressing his grief for the dead French sailors but making clear his views 'that a British defeat would seal for ever his country's bondage'. In September 1940 Churchill backed de Gaulle and Free French forces in an attempt to take Dakar from Vichy France. The failure of this campaign raised doubts in some quarters about Churchill's judgement, with Conservative critics muttering about the Dardanelles. Churchill, although often exasperated to the point of rage by de Gaulle, rightly saw him as a focus for French resistance, outside and inside France. Both men were proud and egotistic, both had a sense of history and both had a firm belief in his own destiny.

Churchill's own destiny was made more secure, above all, by the re-election of Franklin Delano Roosevelt as President of the United States for a third term in November 1940 and by the support, albeit reluctant, of the Chamberlainite Conservatives. With the re-election of Roosevelt, Britain was given vital support by the most powerful nation in a state of heavily-armed ostensible neutrality. At the time of the fall of Chamberlain's government Lloyd George had warned Churchill 'not to allow himself to be converted into an air-raid shelter to keep the splinters from hitting his colleagues'. Churchill, acutely aware of the divisions between the new Lloyd George government of 1916 and the embittered followers of Asquith, went some way into turning Neville Chamberlain into an air-raid shelter for his own political protection, going out of his way to consult and praise the deposed Premier. After Chamberlain's health collapsed, following much consideration he took over the leadership of the Conservative Party on 9 October 1940. Nevertheless, he continued to denounce the former Chamberlainites in private. When he aired such views after the death of Kingsley Wood, his Chancellor of the Exchequer, his Parliamentary Private Secretary, G S Harvie-Watt protested. He later recalled, 'He had no time for the Men of Munich. I was getting tired of that crack, for most of Churchill's government and enthusiastic supporters were Men of Munich. I felt that one by one we would be dropped overboard.' Churchill was in command of the Conservative Party, but tensions remained.

Even in the summer of 1940, when a German invasion of Britain still seemed a major danger, Churchill's thoughts were turning to the defence of the Empire in the Middle East. In August he sent tanks to reinforce Field Marshal Wavell's forces. In this, he out-argued his Chiefs of Staff. The successful outcome, as Andrew Roberts has argued, probably emboldened him later to back his own views against the advice of his senior military advisers sometimes with unfortunate results.[13] Perhaps he did not need encouraging, for as a soldier in the late 1890s he had shown little hesitation in backing his judgement against his superiors. In December 1940, he was vindicated by Wavell's defeat of Italian forces in Libya. He wrote to the Canadian Prime Minister, *I am very glad that we ran the risk in the teeth of the invasion menace of sending our best tanks to this distant battlefield.*

'He {Churchill} had no time for the Men of Munich. I was getting tired of that crack, for most of Churchill's government and enthusiastic supporters were Men of Munich. I felt that one by one we would be dropped overboard.'

G S HARVIE-WATT

Consequences of this victory may be far reaching. We must be worthy of them. To the Australian Prime Minister he reported on *the fine victory by Imperial Armies* and to President Roosevelt, after reporting the success, he observed that *if Italy can be broken our affairs will be more hopeful than they were four or five months ago.*[14] However, Wavell's success was short-lived. In late March and early April 1941 General Erwin Rommel rolled back Wavell's forces, with all but Tobruk of the British gains lost. Churchill was impatient with military leaders who, in his eyes, were not ready to take sufficient risks. In North Africa he sacked Wavell and then General Sir Claude Auchinleck before finding the commander he sought in General Bernard Montgomery (whose success, nevertheless, was to be built on cautious preparation).

As well as the Free French Churchill sought to support Greece, which had been given a British guarantee in March 1939, when Mussolini invaded on 28 October 1940. He was alert to the strategic importance of Crete for the security of Egypt, as well, to a lesser extent, of Greece and the Aegean islands to the eastern Mediterranean. He was also aware of the negative implications of the fall of Greece for possible Turkish intervention in the war and for the Balkans generally. In this he was keener than his military advisers and Anthony Eden.

General (later Field Marshal) **Bernard Law Montgomery** (1887–1976) went on after El Alamein to drive the Axis forces out of North Africa with the Americans, invade Sicily and then take command in France and the Low Countries after D-Day in 1944, crossing the Rhine and taking the German surrender on Lunenberg Heath on 7 May 1945. His victories owed much to careful training, preparation and the assembling of overwhelming force. An abrasive personality and untroubled by any false modesty, Montgomery was described by Churchill as *in defeat, unbeatable, in victory unbearable!*.

However, Egypt remained the priority for scarce resources. In early 1941, with a German invasion of Greece imminent, Eden joined Churchill in seeking to support Greece primarily for reasons of boosting the morale of potential allies. A meeting of the Chiefs of Staff on 10 January took the view that 'the extent and effectiveness of ... aid to the Greeks will be a determining factor in the attitude of Turkey and [would] influence the USA and Russia'.[15] However, the Greeks at first refused help, the Yugoslavs, who resisted the German armies, were swiftly defeated and the bulk of the British forces arrived as the Greek armies faced imminent defeat. By the end of April 1941 50,000 Allied troops were evacuated but 11,500 men and much equipment were captured and 26 ships sunk. As A J P Taylor has commented, 'It was a lesser Dunkirk and all to no purpose. Heart was not put into the freedom-loving nations.'[16]

Worse still, given its strategic importance, was the fall of Crete in May 1941. The British were wrongly confident that British sea power safeguarded it. German airborne forces landed on 20 May. On 23 May Churchill informed Wavell, *Crete battle must be won. Even if enemy secure good lodgments fighting must be maintained indefinitely in the island, thus keeping enemy main striking force tied down to the task.*[17] Four days later, with the lack of air support for British forces, he had to order the evacuation of Crete. By the end of May 16,000 men left the island, leaving 5,000 to surrender. During the short campaign the navy lost three cruisers and six destroyers.

Churchill was brought to his lowest point so far in the war by the bad news from Crete and the simultaneous temporary escape of the German battleship *Bismarck* from its Royal Navy pursuers, having sunk the battlecruiser *Hood* with the loss of some 1,500 lives. John Colville noted in his diaries on 25 May Churchill saying *that these three days had been the worst yet*. He also said that *the loss of half the Mediterranean fleet would be worthwhile in order to save Crete* and, of the Middle East, reverting the pattern of his past (notably Antwerp in 1914), 'If he could be put in command there he would gladly lay down his present office – yes, and even renounce cigars and alcohol!' The following day, after a War Cabinet meeting, Sir Alexander Cadogan of the Foreign Office noted in his diary, 'Poor Winston will recover all right if we get a bit of good news. Tonight he was almost throwing his hand in, but there is a bit of the histrionic art in that.'[18] There was immediate good news to cheer Churchill and to quieten his few critics in the House of Commons, when *Bismarck* was sunk on 27 May. Wavell had also had a success earlier in the month, defeating Italian forces in East Africa and so enabling the Emperor Haile Selassie to return to Abyssinia.

However, the greatest upturns for Churchill and Britain came from the aggressive actions of Germany and Japan. On 22 June 1941 Hitler invaded Russia, nearly 129 years to the day after Napoleon. It led to the death of 20 million people of the Soviet Union and to dire results also for the invading army and the civilians of eastern Germany. Yet it brought Britain its first major ally against Nazi Germany since the fall of France. Churchill made one of his finest broadcasts that evening. His long record as a fervid enemy of Bolshevism gave great credibility to his very moving call to aid the Russian people against Hitler's *mechanised armies* sent to *new fields of slaughter, pillage and devastation*. He began his broadcast by declaring that *we have reached one of the climacterics of the war*. He stated that the earlier of *these intense turning-points* were the fall of France, the Battle of Britain and the US granting Britain resources under its Lend-Lease legislation. He commented, *No one has been a more consistent opponent of Communism than I have for the last twenty-five years. I will unsay no word that I have spoken about it.* He concluded, *The Russian danger is ... our danger, and the danger of the United States, just as the cause of any Russian fighting for his hearth and home is the cause of free men and free peoples in every quarter of the globe.* He also took care to emphasise, *This is no class war, but a war in which the whole British Empire and Commonwealth of Nations is engaged without distinction of race, creed or party.*[19] The Soviet Union was a major ally in Churchill's anti-Nazi coalition, but he still patiently awaited the formation of the decisive Grand Alliance including the might of the United States. Hitler's invasion of Russia consumed massive German resources, thereby taking much pressure off Britain. It lessened fears of a German advance on Iraq's oil fields and it emboldened Auchinleck to take the offensive in North Africa to relieve Tobruk. Rommel withdrew and early in 1942 British forces again reached Benghazi.

> *The Russian danger is ... our danger, and the danger of the United States, just as the cause of any Russian fighting for his hearth and home is the cause of free men and free peoples in every quarter of the globe.*
>
> CHURCHILL

In early 1941 the British had been losing the Battle of the Atlantic. Nearly 700,000 tons of shipping were sunk in April 1941 alone. Churchill told colleagues that such losses were then a greater fear to him than an invasion or the situation in the Balkans. The use of the convoy system greatly improved the situation. Churchill rightly felt that their assembly could not be kept secret but, in a characteristic intervention in details, he declared that *the continued fabrication and dissemination of false information is a necessary part of security.* He added, *All kinds of Munchhausen tales can be spread about to confuse and baffle the truth. Sun helmets or winter clothing should be hawked about ....* In this life-or-death sea struggle Britain was massively helped by Roosevelt who, from November

1940, ordered American warships to patrol the US side of the Atlantic and within a year German U-boars were sinking US ships and being destroyed by them. As A J P Taylor wrote, 'In fact, the United States was conducting an undeclared war at sea against Germany.'[20]

The United States, while not out to provoke war in the Far East, took a firm stance with Japan which was expanding into the vacuum created by the defeat or preoccupation with war of the European imperial powers. The freezing of Japanese assets and the embargo of oil to her undercut the Japanese campaigns in Asia and led to the air attack on Pearl Harbor on 7 December 1941. Earlier, in a speech at the Mansion House, London, on 10 November, Churchill spoke of his voting for the Anglo-Japanese alliance in 1902 and his past admiration for the Japanese, but declared that nevertheless *that, should the United States become involved in war with Japan, the British declaration will follow within the hour*. He sought a reciprocal statement from the US but, as only Congress could declare war, he did not get it. He feared that Japan would attack British territory and embroil Britain, not the US, in a Far Eastern War. Pearl Harbor answered that fear. Churchill at last had his Grand Alliance and the British Empire at the end of 1941, unlike the beginning, was no longer alone. Roosevelt commented on 8 December 1941, 'Today, all of us are in the same boat with you and the people of the Empire – and it is a ship which will not and can not be sunk.'[21]

Chapter 5: Grand Alliance but Gradual Decline, 1941–5

Churchill's finest hour has usually been considered to be in the summer of 1940, but sometimes this 'hour' has been extended to some 18 months, from May 1940 to December 1941. The shorter period is more convincing. Yet, for Britain at war he was near the essential person for longer. Sir Edward Bridges later gave his considered verdict, 'From May 1940 to, say, the middle of 1942 were the greatest years of Churchill's life. Everything depended upon him and upon him alone. Only he had the power to make the nation believe that it could win.'[1] While this may overstate his indispensability, it is roughly right in its recognition that as the main centre of gravity of the war effort moved away from Britain, his importance diminished. British strength ebbed away imperceptibly for a short while but that Britain was increasingly economically dependent on the United States was very visible by the last year of the war.

Britain had never been alone. Its war effort was part of what Sir Charles Dilke in Victoria's reign had called 'Greater Britain'. Liberal Unionists, such as Dilke, Joseph Chamberlain and the imperial pro-consul Sir Alfred Milner, and Liberal Imperialists, such as Lord Rosebery, had believed that the British Empire was the key to Britain remaining a superpower in the 20th century. Churchill throughout his active career espoused the cause of the British Empire. During the Second World War the Empire sustained Britain's war effort, through direct financial help and through the Sterling Area as well as through military assistance.

Yet that could not have been enough, without Roosevelt's provision of massive financial loans, naval assistance and much other aid going well beyond any actions normally associated with neutrality. This was not just a 'special relationship' but an extraordinary relationship, and one which led to the Japanese and German declarations of war on the United States and thereby (on top of the war with the Soviet Union, in Germany's case) to their eventual defeat. Churchill's resilience in 1940–1 owed a huge amount to his conviction of eventual United States participation in the war.

As for Britain, it was to be a victor whose weaknesses had been exposed, especially in the Far East to the Japanese forces. Could Britain have remained a Great Power? This is a question which most probably implies, Could her Empire be maintained? The avoidance of Balance of Power diplomacy with its probable continental European commitments, espoused by Cobdenite Liberals and cautious mid-Victorian Conservatives, was a far from convincing policy by the 1930s. Meeting Nazi Germany's grievances resulted in the Nazi-Soviet Pact in 1939, not the two regimes' mutual elimination. Far from being an isolated imperial power off a Nazi-controlled continental Europe, following German victory in Russia, Britain could have become a greater, fortified German-occupied version of the Channel Islands, facing the Atlantic.

Churchill's greatness lay in identifying the terrible nature of the Nazi ideology and the ever-expansionist dynamics of the Nazi state and recognising that freedom and democracy could not long survive side by side with such a powerful force. John Charmley, when reassessing British options, has written, 'Rather like the Habsburg Empire, Britain could remain a Great Power only by avoiding the war which her more Romantic statesmen imagined would re-establish her in that position'. The Habsburg Monarchy is a good comparison. Given the economic, social and cultural forces in the world, things could only get worse in the mid-20th century for far-flung European empires. But Britain did not fight to re-establish her position, but for national survival and the survival of her culture of freedom and democracy. It was a fight of resistance, as de Gaulle also recognised. For Churchill there was no credible alternative; as, indeed, Chamberlain, Halifax and the other Conservative leaders recognised in 1939.[2] This was also recognised by trade unionists and socialists, who had seen the Fascist and Nazi persecution and murder of such opponents. Moreover, that culture of freedom and democracy did survive, and was thereafter upheld by, among others, 'the English speaking peoples'.

Churchill's own importance was due not only to his recognised leadership qualities but also to the nature of such a coalition government. While initially Labour would have found Halifax as an acceptable replacement to Chamberlain, Churchill nevertheless had cross-party appeal for being an unorthodox Conservative. After May 1940 there was no likelihood of one of the Chamberlainite Conservatives succeeding Churchill should he have died or lost the confidence of the House of Commons. Hostility to them was expressed not only by the Left and by the so-called 'glamour boys', the late 1930s Conservative supporters of Churchill and Eden, but also by some maverick Conservatives, such as Captain Alec Cunningham-Reid, author of *Besides Churchill – Who?* (1942) which denounced the continued presence of 'the Baldwin-Chamberlain gang ... in commanding positions'.[3] Anthony Eden was the main potential successor in the Conservative

Party in Churchill's view, but, as mentioned earlier, Anderson was a further possibility as an ostensibly independent MP.

As for the Labour members of the coalition, Churchill deemed Ernest Bevin the biggest figure. Large in personality, as well as physically, he was as confident as Churchill in his judgements and as brutal occasionally in ensuring he got his way; the erstwhile leader of the Transport and General Workers' Union was another potential leader if Churchill and Eden were killed. Churchill admired his abilities and believed there were 'no defeatist tendencies' in him at all. Churchill usually also had respect for Clement Attlee, the Labour Party leader and Deputy Prime Minister. Attlee chaired meetings in a highly efficient way, unlike Churchill who readily drifted into monologues and digressions. On one occasion Attlee reprimanded Churchill, 'I must remind the Rt Hon. Gentleman that a monologue is not a decision' and put in writing his complaint that Churchill wasted busy ministers' time. An indignant Churchill was told by his cronies, Lord Beaverbrook and Brendan Bracken and his private Secretary, John Colville, that Attlee was right, a view endorsed by his wife, Clementine.[4] Churchill, once famously dismissive of Attlee as *a very modest man* but one who *has much to be modest about*, usually did recognise his abilities and integrity.

'I must remind the Rt Hon. Gentleman that a monologue is not a decision.'

ATTLEE TO CHURCHILL

Perhaps the most surprising politician seen as a potential contender to succeed Churchill was Sir Stafford Cripps, almost the epitome of the type of intellectual socialist Churchill loathed. However, they had both wished to see Chamberlain's government broadened in June 1939 and, after Churchill become Prime Minister, he sent Cripps on an 'exploratory mission' to Moscow. From June 1940 until January 1942

Cripps was British ambassador there. He reaped the new-found popularity of the Soviet Union after Hitler's invasion, but left highly disillusioned with Stalin. He returned a highly popular figure, entering the War Cabinet from February to November 1942. His 1942 mission to India was less success-ful. After that his hour had passed. Perhaps the most surpris-ing aspect of Churchill's relationship with Cripps was that he nominated him for his exclusive The Other Club (but Cripps never attended). This was surprising as Churchill's own club was reserved for those whose company he felt he would enjoy. He notably did not nominate either Sir Edward Bridges or Clement Attlee, both of whom gave him loyal wartime service. The Other Club was created in 1911 by Churchill and F E Smith after they failed to win election to 'The Club' (originally set up by Dr Johnson and others as 'The Literary Club'). Churchill's enthusiasm for it was 'laddish' (to use a current phrase); he ate and drank to excess, and in later life sang in his chauffeur-driven car on his way back to Chartwell. He seems to have seen it as a superior junior officers' mess gathering, a boys' club for ageing males.

Churchill also enjoyed his alcohol and cigars. When Churchill was taken aback at Montgomery's refusal of alcohol with a meal, the general stated that he neither drank nor smoke but was 100 per cent fit. To this Churchill responded that he drank and smoked and was 200 per cent fit. But he was not. By late 1943 he persistently suffered from minor ailments and that December he suffered from pneumonia and a minor heart-attack. He was 69 after all, but his lifestyle had not helped and his continued drinking and smoking did him no good.

He had begun drinking heavily in India. Those new to his circle were often shocked by the amount he drank, much champagne, whisky and brandy. His loyal circle of friends and assistants later recalled that he actually drank far less than supposed. Walter Thompson, for instance, recalled that 'successive visitors would find Mr Churchill with a glass of whisky and soda at his elbow; but more often than not it would be the same drink ...'[5] The truth was probably that he knew when he could afford to indulge and when not to, and so was rarely out of control. It was a bad habit that he passed on to his son, Randolph, and which helped to undermine his political career. Churchill's alleged heavy drinking also attracted adverse comment at high levels in Washington and became a feature of Nazi propaganda. As for the cigars, Churchill, an adroit image-maker, had adopted a cigar as a political trademark early on. Colin Thornton-Kemsley, when recalling Churchill's early days in his Epping constituency, wrote of him appearing 'clad in a fur-lined coat, smoking an expensive cigar', with a private stock of champagne, brandy and cigars in his hotel.[6]

Churchill's dynamism and his generally generous disposition inspired loyalty in those who worked closely with him, but his proneness to interfere and to dominate often exasperated. That he was reviled by Sir Alan Brooke, the Chief of the Imperial General Staff, in his diaries came as a shock to many when they were published partly in 1957 and 1959 and almost fully in 2001. Brooke often had daily rows with Churchill and let off steam in his diary. For instance, on 8 October 1943 he wrote, 'I am slowly becoming convinced that in his old age Winston is becoming less and less well balanced!' Churchill expected those he worked with to defend their views robustly, otherwise he trampled them, and Brooke stood up to him. Brooke noted on 25 February 1944, after a day of lengthy arguing, Churchill summoned him to dine. Far from sacking him, as he half expected, they 'had a tête-à-tête dinner at which he was charming, as if he meant to make up for some of the rough passages of the day. He has astonishing sides to his character.' Nevertheless, Brooke clearly often had doubts about Churchill's judgement, especially in 1944. In particular, he was exasperated in March that Churchill repeatedly pressed for an attack on the tip of Sumatra or Simeulue, which again led him to write on the 17th, 'I am honestly getting very doubtful about his balance of mind'.[7] However, all this was not new. Lloyd George and his two Chiefs of the Imperial General Staff, William Robertson and Henry Wilson, had had stark differences and Wilson had written vitriolically of his Premier in his diaries. It reflected the powerful civil-military friction over command in such wars.

Churchill and Roosevelt had agreed joint war aims even before Pearl Harbor. They had first met during the war (having met briefly in 1918) at Placentia Bay, Newfoundland, from 9 to 12 August 1941. In order to dispel rumours within the US that, as in the First World War, Britain was making secret promises of territory, the two leaders agreed a list of democratic principles. The draft list was drawn up by Sir Alexander Cadogan, the head of the Foreign Office, and revised for Roosevelt by Sumner Welles, Under Secretary in the State Department. The draft was referred to the War Cabinet, which added what became the fifth principle on labour and social issues. The Atlantic Charter, as it became known, contained eight principles: (1) no territorial aggrandisement; (2) no territorial changes without the free consent of the people concerned; (3) the right to self-government; (4) equal access for all to the world's raw materials and equal opportunity to trade; (5) improved labour standards, economic advancement and social security; (6) 'after the destruction of the Nazi tyranny', the securing of a lasting peace; (7) freedom to travel on the high seas; and (8) the abandonment of the use of force, with peace guaranteed by a permanent system of general security.

The implications of the Atlantic Charter raised expectations within the Empire (regarding self-determination) and alarm among the Conservative Right (regarding self-determination and imperial preference in trade). Churchill, when reporting to the House of Commons on 9 September on the charter, stated that it did not *qualify in any way the various statements of policy which have been made from time to time about the development of constitutional government in India, Burma or other parts of the British Empire* and stated that he and Roosevelt had *had in mind, primarily ... nations of Europe now under the Nazi yoke*.[8] To American protests at this, he referred to the implications for the Jews if applied in Palestine and more generally justified it as essential for internal British politics. The Atlantic Charter was endorsed at the White House on 1 January 1942 by 26 countries, with a further 22 signing later. These 48 countries became the nucleus of the United Nations in April–June 1945.

On 10 November 1942, a year after Churchill's speech at the Mansion House in which he declared Britain would declare war on Japan if she attacked the United States, he proudly proclaimed the battle of El Alamein (October–November 1942) to be a great British Empire victory, noting in particular the part played by Indian troops, and making his famous remark, *Now this is not the end. It is not even the beginning of the end. But it is, perhaps, the end of the beginning*. This message was combined with him consolidating his support among the Empire-minded Conservatives and making his position clear to the Americans. He stated *We*

We mean to hold our own. I have not become the King's First Minister in order to preside over the liquidation of the British Empire.

CHURCHILL

have not entered this war for profit or expansion but only for honour and to do our duty in defending the right. He went on, *We mean to hold our own. I have not become the King's First Minister in order to preside over the liquidation of the British Empire,* and made it clear he would resign and precipitate a general election before doing so.[9]

Before El Alamein Churchill had very few successes but many disasters to report. The sending of the battleship *Prince of Wales* and the battlecruiser *Repulse* to the Far East without adequate aircraft cover ended in both ships being sunk on 10 December 1941, with the loss of 600 men. It was a loss especially bitter as he had travelled aboard the *Prince of Wales* to the conference at Placentia Bay. He had ordered the battleships to the Far East. As David Reynolds has commented, 'The decision reveals two of his greatest errors as a strategist – underestimation of Japan and complacency about naval airpower.'[10] The loss of the two ships ensured the loss of Singapore and Malaya, on top of that earlier of Hong Kong. The surrender of Singapore on 15 February 1942 was the nadir of the British war effort and a massive blow to British imperial prestige in Asia. It was followed by the loss of Burma in April 1942. Japanese dominance of the Pacific Ocean, however, was broken by the American victory at Midway on 4 June 1942. British support for Russia was limited to providing supplies by convoys to Archangel, with the loss of some 100 ships, and by bomber raids on Germany. Churchill wisely resisted a premature invasion of Europe, in spite of Stalin's repeated demands for the Second Front. Marshall Zhukov and the Red Army ended, then reversed, German expansion eastwards at Stalingrad in late 1942 and early 1943, with 91,000 German troops surrendering by 2 February.

In early 1943 Churchill still counted as much as Stalin in the Grand Alliance. At the Casablanca Conference in January

1943 Churchill succeeded in securing US agreement not to invade northern Europe in 1943 but to follow up victory in North Africa with the invasion of Sicily. The meeting was followed by combined planning in London for the invasion of northern Europe in 1944. They also planned more action against German U-boats, an intensification of bombing of Germany and the recovery of Burma. Roosevelt publicly announced the Allied war aim of securing unconditional surrender from Germany, Italy and Japan. Churchill had favoured omitting Italy from the list, *to encourage a break-up there*, but the War Cabinet unanimously called for its inclusion. Later in the war, Churchill avoided taking action to oust Franco from Spain.[11] He had earlier spoken of the Spanish people deserving peace after the Spanish Civil War.

Roosevelt, Churchill and their advisers met again in Quebec in August 1943. By this time the Allied invasion of Sicily had discredited Mussolini. The imminent collapse of his regime encouraged the Allies to invade mainland Italy, while the Germans took over Rome. This ensured that the Second Front in northern Europe was delayed until 1944, to the wrath of Stalin whose forces took the offensive after the great tank battle of Kursk in July. Quebec also saw Anglo-American agreement to share atomic information.

By the time of the Tehran Conference of November–December 1943 Britain was increasingly financially dependent on the United States. British forces fought valiantly, but were increasingly reliant on US-supplied equipment. At Tehran Churchill discovered he was not as big as the Big Two. His joke afterwards was very pointed: *There I sat with the great Russian bear on one side*

There I sat with the great Russian bear on one side … and on the other side the great American buffalo, and between the two sat the poor little English donkey.

CHURCHILL

... and on the other side the great American buffalo, and between the two sat the poor little English donkey.[12] In fact Stalin and Roosevelt began their first meeting an hour before Churchill joined them. Stalin secured firm promises of a 1944 invasion of northern France and recognition of Tito as the major resistance leader in Yugoslavia. Churchill and Roosevelt were pleased to receive a pledge from Stalin that he would declare war on Japan after the defeat of Germany. More ominous for the future were discussions on new frontiers for Poland.

On 6 June 1944 American and British Empire forces landed in Normandy. On 12 June Churchill, Brooke and Smuts crossed the Channel and were met on the beach by Montgomery and several jeeps, and were taken to his headquarters. Churchill, as usual, was thrilled to be near military action, albeit for only a day. By the time of the second Quebec Conference, September 1944, again between Churchill, Roosevelt and their advisers, the British were heavily financially dependent on the United States. Colville noted in his diary, 'The Conference has been going exceedingly well from our point of view and the Americans are being amenable both strategically and financially.'[13] The Americans agreed to the British fleet joining theirs in the central Pacific and to the British setting about recovering Burma. Churchill and Roosevelt agreed to further bombing of Germany. There was also discussion of post-war occupation zones in Germany and Churchill and Roosevelt agreed to the plans of Henry Morgenthau, US Secretary of the Treasury, to de-industrialise Germany (but these were subsequently dropped, with the British War Cabinet hostile and Roosevelt reversing his agreement).

Having had bipartite talks with Roosevelt, Churchill made the hazardous journey to Moscow in October 1944 to speak with Stalin. They discussed at length the future frontiers of

Poland and spheres of influence in the Balkans. Stalin readily agreed to Churchill's suggestion of Britain having prime influence in Greece and half influence in Yugoslavia and Hungary, while Russia should have predominant influence in Romania and Bulgaria. Stalin also wanted Germany's heavy industry destroyed and the country split in order to prevent another war of revenge.

At the Yalta conference, 3–11 February 1945, when Churchill, Roosevelt and Stalin were together again, it was even more apparent than at Tehran that Churchill had slid further in status, there now being only a Big Two. With the Red Army only 40 miles from Berlin, the Allies needed to elaborate on matters initially agreed at Tehran. There were further discussions on the future of Poland, arrangements for the occupation of Germany and Austria and on Russia joining the war against Japan. The three leaders agreed to the 'Declaration on Liberated Europe', which pledged their countries to help those newly-freed nations 'to solve by democratic means their pressing political and economic problems'. The optimism of Yalta was short-lived. Churchill was almost immediately doubtful as to Stalin's good faith concerning Poland. After Roosevelt died and was succeeded on 12 April 1945 by Harry S Truman, the new president was briefed that 'the British government has been showing increasing apprehension of Russia and her intentions'.[14]

A few days after Yalta, on 13 and 14 February 1945, the RAF bombed Dresden, with horrific results. The Casablanca Conference in January 1943 had agreed on British and American bombing of key industrial targets. At the Quebec Conference Churchill had eagerly shown Stalin photographs of the effects of British bombing, as proof of British endeavours while the Red Army took the brunt of German military power. Dresden was bombed after British, American and

Russian chiefs of staff on 5 February 1945 agreed to bomb this and other cities in the region to break German communications when German divisions were being brought to the Eastern Front. By the time of Dresden such bombing was being questioned in Britain both for its effectiveness as a use of resources and as to its morality. Arthur Harris, commander in chief of Bomber Command, had come to believe that area bombing, rather than precision bombing, would win the war. Churchill had been used to retaliatory action in the army, himself engaging in the laying waste of villages and crops on the North-West Frontier of India. He also shared British popular sentiments that the Germans should be given a taste of what London, Coventry, Plymouth and other British cities had suffered during the Blitz and were still suffering as a result of V2 missiles. However, the terrible firestorms and 25,000 or more deaths in Dresden were seen in Britain as unacceptable, not least as the war was coming to an end. Air Chief Marshal Arthur Harris and Bomber Command were the least praised of the British fighting forces at the end of the war and the request for a medal for Bomber Command was refused. However, Churchill complained when Harris was omitted from Attlee's honours lists and Harris declined Churchill's 1951 offer of a peerage but did accept a baronetcy in 1953.

Whether or not Churchill and the RAF could and should have done more about the concentration camps is still debated. In the case of Auschwitz when, in July 1944, Chaim Weitzman called for the bombing of the railway lines to the camp, Churchill told Eden *Get anything out of the Air Force you can, and invoke me if necessary*, and he agreed to using the press and radio to publicise what was being done to Hungarian Jews there. Churchill also informed Eden four days later that all involved in such crimes should be executed, observing, *There is no doubt that this is probably the greatest and most horrible crime ever committed in the whole history of the world, and it has been done by scientific machinery by nominally civilised men in the name of a great State and one of the leading races of Europe.*[15]

The German instrument of surrender was signed in the early hours of 7 May 1945 and came into effect at one minute after midnight on 8/9 May. Churchill broadcast a victory speech at 3 p.m. on 8 May in which he warned *Japan, with all her treachery and greed, remains unsubdued*, and called for *justice and retribution* for *her detestable crimes*. He then addressed the House of Commons, attended a service of Thanksgiving, saw the King at Buckingham Palace and they stood on the balcony there, then he twice addressed huge crowds from the balcony of the Ministry of Health in Whitehall. These were his hours of triumph.

This is not a victory of a party or any class. It's a victory of the great British nation as a whole.

CHURCHILL

Churchill was magnanimous and expansive in his praise on 8 May. He told the cheering crowds, *This is not a victory of a party or any class. It's a victory of the great British nation as a whole.* He had Bevin (and Anderson) flanking him on the balcony at Buckingham Palace. Yet, when the Labour Party conference called for a return to party politics in the 1945 general election, Churchill foolishly came off the high ground and exercised his powerful rhetoric on his erstwhile loyal Labour ministerial colleagues. He set the tone in his first election broadcast on 4 June in which he reverted to his earlier anti-Bolshevik rhetoric. He declared, *A Free Parliament is odious to the Socialist doctrinaire*, and linked this point to Herbert Morrison and Sir Stafford Cripps. He went on to say *no Socialist system can be established without a political police ... They would have to fall back on some form of Gestapo*, and warned that their policies *would destroy the value of any scrap of savings or nest-egg that anyone had accumulated in this country.*[16] His own daughter Sarah, no welfare dependant, praised his intentions but observed, 'Socialism as practised in the war did no one any harm and quite a lot of people good. The children of this country have never been so well fed or healthy ...'[17]

The Labour leadership was not a group of British Lenins, but, as Paul Addison, has put it, 'essentially moderate social patriots' and during the Second World War 'an aristocrat steeped in a romantic vision of his nation's role was the undisputed leader of an overwhelmingly working-class nation of whose social conditions and daily concerns he was largely in ignorance'.[18] While Churchill was personally immensely popular, his disparagement of the Labour leaders was not nor was his lack of enthusiasm for William Beveridge's welfare proposals. When the results of the general election became known on 26 July, Labour, with 393 seats, had a majority of 146 while the Conservatives had only 213 seats. Churchill resigned immediately.

Sir William Beveridge's report on Social Insurance and Allied Services, published in December 1942, laid the basis for the modern Welfare State. Arguing that government should fight the 'five giants' of 'want, disease, ignorance, squalor and idleness', it proposed a free-at-point-of-use health service, unemployment benefits and death grants to pay funeral costs, funded out of a compulsory National Insurance scheme. The wartime government accepted the recommendations of the report in February 1943, and after the 1945 election the Attlee government set about putting them into practice, and later Conservative governments would continue the wartime consensus on the Welfare State.

Chapter 6: Cold War and The End of Empire, 1945–65

Churchill's second period as Prime Minister, 1951–5, was a result of his leadership in the Second World War and his determination that his career would not end with the rejection at the polls in 1945. Perhaps anyway, his career would have gone on until his party, the electorate or Clementine and his family called time on it. Like William Gladstone who had spent 20 years repeatedly proclaiming his desire to retire, Churchill wished to go on and on at the top of British politics. He often explicitly measured his political longevity against that of the Victorian statesman, much as Tony Blair was alert to Margaret Thatcher's longevity as premier.

Churchill, like Lloyd George and Ramsay MacDonald before him and Eden, Macmillan, Douglas-Home, Thatcher and Blair after him, was convinced that he alone had the prestige to make a difference for Britain at what became known as summit conferences. He had been at the Potsdam Conference, with Roosevelt and Truman, as well as Attlee, before the 1945 election results were announced. There he had been involved in discussions about the continuing war with Japan, securing free elections in Greece, Allied control of Germany and Austria and the freedom of Greece, Persia and Turkey. He was also informed of the United States' first atomic bomb test in New Mexico. Perhaps his greatest regret in losing the general election was the loss of his top seat at the conference table when the post-war international settlement was being discussed.

After the loss of the election became apparent, Clementine Churchill offered the consolatory thought, 'It may be a blessing in disguise'. To this he made his famous riposte, *Well, at the moment it's certainly very well disguised.* After being the hub of world-important, ceaseless activity, he was left with an emptiness. As his daughter has commented, 'The Map room was deserted; the Private Office empty; no official telegrams; no "red boxes".' For a while at home he was like a bear with a sore head, but recovered somewhat with a holiday at Lake Como and much painting.[1]

The years of opposition gave Churchill the time to work on his study in six volumes, *The Second World War* (1948–53). As David Reynolds has argued in his analysis of the writing of these volumes, he used them to secure his wartime reputation and to make firm his case for a further period as Prime Minister. 'To do so meant running the equivalent of an academic research group while also acting as Leader of the Opposition and a globe-trotting international statesman.'[2] As Leader of the Opposition he dumped much on Anthony Eden, generally adopting the relaxed attitude to leadership that Disraeli had taken when Churchill was born.

In writing his version of the Second World War Churchill was skilful in often slanting his past performances to the needs of post-1945 international relations. He was keen to show himself firmer for the invasion of northern France than he had been at the time (when he prioritised Italy), he downplayed his fluctuating attitudes towards Stalin and the Soviet Union, post-war events being less suggestive of the manageability of Stalin, and he omitted to stress the economic and manpower exhaustion of Britain in the last nine months or so of the war (Lindemann, for instance, talking of Britain facing 'an Economic Dunkirk' in February 1945).[3] He also was diplomatic in his references to foreign leaders still in power such as General Eisenhower and Tito.

After 1945 Churchill continued to proclaim his belief in the Empire but he also made much of the 'English Speaking Peoples', meaning the US and the British and British Empire. In 1940 he had pressed for common citizenship in France and, briefly, after 1945 he even talked of the possibility of common United States and British citizenship. More often he spoke of the solidarity of *the English-speaking world* which he believed *can weather all storms that blow*.[4] In 1953 he dusted off his draft of *The History of the English Speaking Peoples* which he had completed in 1939. After thorough revision, the first volume was published in 1956 with a Preface in which Churchill wrote, *Vast numbers of people on both sides of the Atlantic and throughout the British Commonwealth of Nations have felt a sense of brotherhood.* He wanted such feelings fostered, but argued such developments did not exclude other developments such as *the erection of structures like United Europe.* He commented, *There is a growing feeling that the English-speaking peoples might point a finger showing the way if things went right, and could of course defend themselves ... if things went wrong.*[5]

For a few years after the Second World War Churchill was enthusiastic about European Union. It followed on from his Anglo-French endeavours of 1940 and that after 1945, as after 1918, he was more anxious about Russia than Germany. In a major speech at Zurich on 19 September 1946 he made it clear that he saw the British Empire, like the United States and the Soviet Union, as *friends and sponsors of the new Europe.* He observed, *There can be no revival of Europe without a spiritually great France and a spiritually great Germany.*[6] His prime interest in a united Western Europe was in defence, with economic

Churchill's Zurich Speech, 19 September 1945

Churchill's speech at Zurich on 19 September 1946 caused a sensation in calling for a united Europe with Germany a crucial part of such a development. As a result he was seen as a key figure in the early days of the European Movement. However, Churchill's thinking was very much affected by the early Cold War. He warned that such a European grouping should be built quickly, while only the United States had atomic weapons. He saw the united Europe as principally a western European grouping. He made it clear that 'we British have our own Commonwealth of Nations'. So he envisioned a united Europe that would be defensively relatively strong, reliant on US nuclear protection and would become part of the existing 'natural grouping in the western hemisphere', then resting on 'the English speaking peoples'.

'And what is the plight to which Europe has been reduced? Some of the smaller states indeed made a good recovery, but over wide areas a vast quivering mass of tortured, hungry, careworn and bewildered human beings gape at the ruins of their cities and homes, and scan the dark horizon for the approach of some new peril, tyranny or terror ...

... Yet all the while there is a remedy which, if it were generally and spontaneously adopted, would as if by a miracle transform the whole scene, and would in a few years make all Europe, or the greater part of it, as free and as happy as Switzerland is today. What is this sovereign remedy? It is to recreate the European Family, or as much of it as we can, and provide it with a structure under which it can dwell in peace, in safety and freedom. We must build a kind of united states of Europe ...

... The first step in the re-creation of the European Family must be a partnership between France and Germany. In this way only can France recover the moral leadership of Europe. There can be no revival of Europe without a spiritually great France and spiritually great Germany.'

growth second. While Churchill continued to be a sponsor of the United Europe movement, it was not a priority when he returned to government, not least as it was an issue that already divided the Conservative Party. While his European speeches attracted great attention, his most influential speech of these years was that given at Fulton, Missouri, on 5 May 1946, which became known as his 'Iron Curtain' speech.

At Fulton Churchill spoke of the role of 'the English-speaking peoples' in the post-war world and their need to play their part in shielding people from war and tyranny. To prevent war he hoped all countries would contribute to a United Nations armed force. For the prevention of war and tyranny, Churchill called for the development of *a special relationship between the British Commonwealth and Empire and the United States of America* and argued that it was essential for the UN to be effective. He spoke warmly of Stalin and the Russian people's struggle against Germany but then remarked, *From Stettin in the Baltic to Trieste in the Adriatic, an iron curtain has descended across the Continent* and said of the Soviet sphere, *this is certainly not the liberated Europe we fought to build up*. He went on to warn of countries such as France and Italy where *the Communist parties or fifth columns constitute a growing challenge and peril to Christian civilisation*. He suggested of the leaders of the Soviet Union that *there is nothing they admire so much as strength* and urged the United States and the British Empire to be prepared, unlike many politicians of the 1930s. Yet he insisted, *I repulse the idea that a new war is inevitable*.[7]

> *From Stettin in the Baltic to Trieste in the Adriatic, an iron curtain has descended across the Continent.*
>
> CHURCHILL

Churchill's speech aroused massive press and public interest around the world. Churchill had been airing the major themes in it since autumn 1945. Its warm reception by many in the

United States was due to him publicly stating what policy makers were privately writing and President Truman had begun to indicate already in a major speech in October 1945. The speech was neither a surprise nor unwelcome to Attlee and Bevin, Britain's Prime Minister and Foreign Secretary.[8]

Perhaps the least commented-on feature of Churchill's Fulton speech was his talking-up the global importance of the British Empire. This was the obverse side of the last volume of *The Second World War* where he nearly brushed out of his picture Britain's economic weakness towards the end of the war. At Fulton he referred to the British post-war problems of restarting industries, recovering export markets and coping with rationing and predicted that in 50 years time the Americans would *see 70 or 80 millions of Britons spread about the world and united in defence of our traditions, our way of life, and the world causes which you and we espouse*. While warning of Communism, his final message to the American political elite was that *an overwhelming assurance of security* would come if the British Empire and the United States were joined in *fraternal association*. At Fulton Churchill was trying to use US concerns about the Soviet Union to cement the Anglo-American wartime alliance. Churchill moved from continuing to make expressions of goodwill towards Stalin (which he did as late as January 1947) to talking in late 1947 and early 1948 of giving him an ultimatum to make a reasonable post-war territorial settlement or face a pre-emptive nuclear strike if he failed to do so. As John Young has observed, this was a highly dangerous approach, even given Churchill's confidence that Stalin would settle.[9]

By the time of the 1950 general election Churchill had turned from nuking the Russians if they were uncooperative to offering a return to summit diplomacy. At Edinburgh on 14 February he said, *The idea appeals to me of a supreme effort to bridge the gulf between the two worlds, so that each can live their life, if not in friendship at least without the hatreds of the cold war.* He added, *It is not easy to see how things could be worsened by a parley at the summit.*[10] Churchill continued to have hopes of top-table negotiations while in opposition, though the Korean War lessened his expectations and his talk of summit diplomacy.

In Opposition the Conservative Party rebuilt its organisation and revised its policies. In particular it made an appeal to industrial working people with its *Industrial Charter*. R A Butler, not Churchill, was the driving force behind this. However, Churchill was very happy to speak the language of Tory democracy again. At the 1947 Conservative Party conference he declared, *It was the trade unions whom Benjamin Disraeli and the Conservative Party gave strong support to in 1875 ... The trade unions are a long-established and essential part of our national life ... we take our stand by these pillars of our British society as it has gradually been developed and evolved itself, of the right of individual labouring men to adjust their wages and conditions by collective bargaining, including the right to strike.*[11]

> **Richard Austen ('Rab') Butler** (1902–82) was Minister of Education in the wartime government, and brought in the 1944 Education Act which introduced free primary and secondary education for all. He was Chancellor of the Exchequer in Churchill's second government, and deputised for the Prime Minister when he was ill. Always thought to be a future prime minister himself, he never made it, losing out to Macmillan in 1957, whose Home Secretary he was, and Sir Alec Douglas-Home in 1963. He retired from the Commons in 1965 and went to the Lords as Baron Butler of Saffron Walden.

However, such sentiments did not stop Churchill in the general elections of 1950 and 1951 from letting rip at socialism. Early on in the 1950 campaign, in Cardiff, when as in 1945 he wished to make vehement anti-socialist senti-ments, he quoted Lloyd George. Elsewhere he used his own words when denouncing socialism, as in 1945 and earlier. In his Edinburgh speech on 14 February he attacked 'Fair shares for all' as equal shares for all: *Equal shares for those who toil and those who shirk. Equal shares for those who save and those who squander. No reward offered to the skilled craftsman*, and much more of the same. At Chingford the next day he began on the theme *Socialism is a preliminary stage to Communism, and Communism is the accomplishment of Socialism*. In the 1951 general election he was a little more circumspect but raised the bogey of *Bevanite Socialism*, which he deemed in spite of its intentions would increase *the hazard of a world catastrophe*.[12]

In the 1951 general election Churchill won a majority of seats, but with less votes than Labour, and returned to 10 Downing Street. His final government has been controversial for several reasons, but above all because of differing views as to his physical fitness for the post. He had had a stroke while staying at Beaverbrook's villa in the south of France in August 1949, which had been hushed up as 'a chill'. The morality of concealing information concerning this from his party and the electorate was dubious. What was outrageous was the array of subterfuges employed to disguise his serious stroke on 23 June 1953 when he was Prime Minister, with Butler and Lord Salisbury removing mention of 'a disturbance of cerebral circulation' from a press bulletin. The House of Commons, not surprisingly, was very taken aback on 2 March 1955 when, angered by criticism made by Aneurin Bevan, he referred to *a very sudden illness which paralysed me completely* while running a hand down his left arm and leg.[13]

At the time Churchill's justification for carrying on was that Eden, his successor, had had a major operation on 23 June, and so he informed the Queen he hoped to hold on until the autumn when Eden could succeed him. He conceded to Opposition demands that Salisbury should be appointed Acting Foreign Secretary while Eden recuperated. However, as Churchill's daughter Mary later noted, 'as his strength increased, the "holding on" theme was more and more superseded by the idea of "carrying on"'.[14] However, in 1954 and early 1955 even Churchill's adulatory entourage and 'Secret Circle' of civil servants were recognising his physical decline while they did much to enable him to struggle on. Just as Gladstone had tormented Hartington and, later, other colleagues with his talk of retiring before long, but with the crucial date repeatedly moving forward, so Churchill exasperated Eden and his other colleagues.

Like Gladstone, Churchill had his mission which he believed only he could achieve. In Gladstone's case it was Home Rule for Ireland, in Churchill's it was to uphold and strengthen 'the special relationship' with the United States and to achieve *détente* with the Soviet Union. Yet while this was the major political motivation for his continuation, the bottom line was that he suffered from the political equivalent of being an alcoholic. He craved political power, the ability to affect events and to hold public attention. When Violet Bonham Carter, who shared his addiction to politics, spoke to him in July 1960 he said that since he had left office, *I have no appetite for life*.[15] Politics had taken over his life in nearly as powerful a way as in fiction the ring took over Gollum in J R R Tolkien's *Lord Of The Rings* (published 1954–5).

With Britain much weakened economically and militarily, Churchill still sought to have major international influence. Although India had received its independence, he still believed that the British Commonwealth and Empire carried weight. He was also very hesitant in letting more go. Churchill's view of much of the Middle East remained coloured by his experiences in the Sudan in late 1890s and as Colonial Secretary after the First World War. He still used the rhetoric of Victorian imperialism; for instance, regretting that Attlee's government had not held Abadan, whereas if he had been in office *there might have been a splutter of musketry*. Yet, as Roger Louis has shown, Churchill was more flexible than his remarks suggested. In the case of Egypt, in spite of all his previous denunciations of 'scuttle', in 1954 he did support a negotiated withdrawal of British forces but with an agreement for their return in the event of a major war.[16]

Earlier, Eden had had to push hard to carry out in 1952 a pledge he had made the previous autumn to give self-government to the Sudan. Churchill, concerned that the Egyptians would seize the Sudan and influenced by his past, was at first equivocal, with Eden later recalling, 'I should have had to resign if I had not got my way' and observing that it 'was one of the rare occasions where I differed from Sir Winston Churchill on a matter of foreign policy'.[17] Nevertheless, there was persistent tension between them as Churchill often acted as if he was his own Foreign Secretary.

Churchill returned to office to uphold and even strengthen Britain's relationship with the United States. While both Presidents Truman and Eisenhower liked Churchill as a person, both were unimpressed by his presumption of a continuing 'special relationship'. Dean Acheson, the US Secretary of State 1949–52, was airing the views of many senior American government figures when he said that Churchill was still 'thinking back to … World War II'. Eisenhower was even more irritated by Churchill's presumption that Anglo-US relations were still in their 1941–5 state. Even before becoming President he wrote of Churchill, 'He simply will not think in terms of today, but rather only those of the war years … My regretful opinion is that the Prime Minister no

Churchill's Premiership

On his return to Number 10, Churchill wanted as many of his old wartime team with him as possible, and his bizarre wartime administrative habits returned too. He would work deep into the night reading the first editions of the national newspapers and firing off biting minutes to unbriefed ministers on whatever claims the *Daily Express* and the other papers might be making about the people's diet or housing. He refrained, however, from attaching his famous red 'Action This Day' labels to these broadsides, even though the Number 10 messengers had carefully put them back on the Cabinet table on the day of his restoration.

Unless the Cabinet or a Cabinet Committee he chaired was due to meet, Churchill would lie in bed until shortly before lunch, an unlit cigar in his mouth, his bed covered in papers, a 'Garden Girl' beside it to take dictation. At his feet would be Rufus the poodle and on his head sat Toby the budgerigar. Toby, for some reason, was particularly excited by the presence of Rab Butler, the Chancellor of the Exchequer. If Rab was briefing Churchill on the latest strains on the economy, Toby would fly around the room, occasionally opening his bowels on Rab's head. On one occasion Butler was seen to mop his head 'with a spotless silk handkerchief' and was head to sigh resignedly, 'The things I do for England ...'

Quite often Churchill would return to No. 10 for the nap which was the fulcrum of his day-and-night work routine. 'Undressed fully apart from a long silk vest, he would take a very small sleeping pill and go to bed for one or two hours, awaking refreshed and ready for dinner or work.' When he went to bed properly he rarely had a sleepless night: *I just turn out the light, say 'bugger everyone', and go to sleep*, he once explained to an inquisitive private secretary. All in all, it was a rich, eccentric, selfish (in terms of its demands on the time of ministers and officials) and shamelessly personal way of heading a government. [Hennessy, *The Prime Minister*, pp 181–3.]

longer absorbs new ideas'. In 1953 he commented of Churchill to his senior colleagues, 'He is just a little Peter Pan'.[18]

Churchill, still reasonably fit in 1951, prioritised seeing Truman and having free-ranging talks on international issues. He felt that Britain could moderate US hostility to the Soviet Union and that eventually he could get a return to Great Men doing business with each other at a summit conference. Churchill and Eden visited Washington from 5 to 19 January 1952. Churchill put on his usual charismatic performance, somewhat like an aged thespian in one of his last appearances, giving vent to his emotions, moving from histrionics to tears. Truman mostly kept cool under Churchill's blandishments. Churchill, convinced that Labour had let Britain down over Anglo-US atomic weapons policy, found that they had not. There was no possibility after the United States 1946 McMahon Act, of sharing atomic secrets, as had been agreed at the 1943 Quebec conference. The reality was that the Americans would only be influenced in operational and other matters if Britain had its own atomic weapons or if it denied them the East Anglian bases. In this conference the issue of British sovereignty raised by these bases was resolved by the formula that American use of the bases 'in an emergency would be a matter for a joint decision … in the light of the circumstances prevailing at the time'; a formula relied on by successive British governments until the end of the Cold War. Similarly, Churchill, full of British naval traditions, tried unsuccessfully to reverse Labour's agreement that under NATO a United States Admiral would be in command of the North Atlantic.[19] As with his jeers of 'scuttle', he found that Attlee and Bevin had been responding to the realities of Britain's diminished international strength. His government later took the decision to develop British nuclear weapons in order to recover some leverage in Anglo-American relations as well as for purely defence reasons.

At the January 1952 Washington conference Truman made it clear that he was not interested in a summit meeting, not least as Stalin had not responded to an invitation to visit Washington. After Eisenhower was elected to succeed Truman, Churchill quickly pressed for a private meeting and was granted one before his inauguration. While Eisenhower, like Truman, was happy to confirm privately that he saw Britain as the United States' closest ally, he also made clear that he was not going to alienate other friendly states by proclaiming this. Moreover, Eisenhower followed Truman in being unwilling to underwrite the British Empire in the Middle East while Churchill continued to be cool on the subjects of a European Defence Community and on US belligerency towards China.

Although the Americans did not share his enthusiasm for summits, Churchill continued to believe that he could and should do business with the Soviet Union. Before Stalin's death on 5 March 1953, Churchill was insistent that he was the best Soviet leader with whom to do business. After his death, as David Carlton has put it, 'Churchill predictably interpreted every subsequent news item relating to the Soviets in a way that favoured his thesis and bolstered his hopes'.[20] Eisenhower, however, wrote to Churchill on 11 March doubting 'the wisdom of a formal multilateral meeting since this would give our opponent the opportunity to block reasonable moves by the West and to make it a propaganda occasion'.[21]

That Eisenhower did not want a summit conference did not stop Churchill from pressing ever more eagerly for one. With Eden seriously ill and then recuperating from April to October 1953, Churchill was free of one domestic restraint.

In Glasgow on 17 April 1953 he detected his own wind of change, asking, *Is there a new breeze blowing on the tormented world?*. He spoke both of another chance possibly coming for the Second World War allies to secure a just and lasting peace as well as the crucial role in this of *the abiding fellowship and brotherhood of the English-speaking world*.[22] The following month he alarmed many in London as well as in Washington by talking of going to Moscow on his own.

Churchill then decided to appeal to public opinion, much as Gladstone used to do when he was not getting his way with his colleagues. He did so in a major speech on foreign affairs in the House of Commons on 11 May, in which he invoked the spirit behind the Locarno Treaty of 1925 which he deemed *the highest point we reached between the wars*. He stated, *We have been encouraged by a series of amicable gestures on the part of the new Soviet government* and observed that it would be *a mistake to assume that nothing can be settled with Soviet Russia unless or until everything is settled*. He therefore said, … *I believe that a conference on the highest level should take place between the leading Powers without long delay. This conference should not be overhung by a ponderous or rigid agenda … The conference should be confined to the smallest number of Powers and persons possible. It should meet with a measure of informality and still greater measure of privacy and seclusion.*[23] According to Gallup polls, Churchill's idea of a summit received overwhelming popular support in both the US and the UK.

The French government's response was to ask Eisenhower for a Western summit meeting of the United States, Britain and France. Churchill, who believed this could be a first step to a summit with the Russians, readily agreed but successfully pressed it be held in Bermuda not in the USA. The conference was arranged for 8 July. Churchill was at a new high, making a big splash in international relations and taking the lead in the 'special relationship' (though in such unilateral action he was doing it no good). However, his stroke on 23 June forced him to ask for the postponement of the Bermuda conference. Instead the British asked for, and got, a meeting of foreign ministers in Washington, with Salisbury going. At this the notion of a summit conference involving the Soviet Union was quickly dismissed until such time as the Soviet Union gave proof in advance of its good faith.

Churchill's own test of whether he could continue as Prime Minister was whether he could address the Conservative Party Conference in October. He did so, and devoted a substantial part of his speech to international affairs and stated of his summit policy that *though we have not yet been able to persuade our trusted allies to adopt it in the form I suggested no one can say that it is dead.* He also commented, *If I stay on for a time being bearing the burden at my age it is not because of love for power or office*, but because *I may ... have an influence on what I care above all else, the building of a sure and lasting peace.* However, a month later he gratuitously offended the Soviet Union and displayed that his memory was unreliable when, speaking at a presentation of a portrait of Clementine Churchill at a school in his constituency, he wrongly claimed to have instructed Field Marshal Montgomery in 1945 to prepare surrendered German weaponry for reissue to German troops if Soviet forces kept advancing.[24]

After the Soviet Union's terms for an East-West foreign ministers' meeting were deemed by America and Britain to be unacceptable, Churchill successfully pressed for the postponed Bermuda meeting to be held in December 1953. However, before this took place the Soviet Union reversed its position on a foreign ministers' meeting and so the Bermuda conference discussed what the Western response should be. At it Churchill was rude to the French and still insisted on trying to resurrect dead issues, most notably seeking US military support for the Suez Canal. John Young has written of his performance at Bermuda, 'His behaviour was very much that of a man in decline, opinionated, inflexible, living in the past, on whom arteriosclerosis had already taken a heavy toll.'[25] All but Churchill were opposed to new approaches to the Soviet Union, and even he saw the hopelessness of a summit in the near future. After Bermuda, Churchill gave his attention to advocating more East-West trade.

In his final premiership Churchill appears to have been especially sensitive to Opposition criticism, over reacting on several occasions. Usually he could pulverise the Opposition. However, on 5 April 1954, when responding to an Opposition motion calling for a summit to deal with the danger of nuclear weapons, Churchill revealed in some detail the secret 1943 Quebec Agreement in order to denounce Attlee. In so doing he outraged many on his own side, as well as the Opposition and was rescued by Eden.

While Eden was far from being alone in hoping Churchill would now retire, Churchill went to Washington in June 1954 still seeking his Holy Grail of a summit conference. Churchill pressed Eisenhower to agree that he, Churchill, should hold a meeting with the Soviet leadership. Churchill, without consulting his Cabinet colleagues (other than Eden), enquired of Molotov whether the Soviet leadership would welcome a meeting with him. This nearly led to the resignation of Salisbury and other ministers. Churchill was exposed as being duplicitous in evading Cabinet consideration of an important act of foreign policy and, according to the Cabinet minutes, admitted 'in his anxiety to lose no opportunity of furthering the cause of world peace, he might have taken an exaggerated view of the urgency of the matter'.[26] For nearly three weeks in July there was a possibility that his government could collapse over his actions, the crisis ending when Churchill gave up immediate hopes of a Moscow meeting. By early 1955 even Churchill had realised that he was not going to have a meaningful Anglo-Soviet conference let alone an East-West summit as the Cold War took a turn for the worse.

Churchill took less interest in domestic policy, his 'mission' being confined to international affairs. His approach to domestic issues was not confrontational. Indeed, later historians and economists have attributed part of the blame for Britain's increasing inflation and lack of competitiveness in export markets to the Churchill government's policies. Such claims have an element of truth, yet they have the benefit of the hindsight of knowing the Conservatives were to win bigger majorities in the House of Commons in both the 1955 and 1959 elections. Conservative policy in 1951–5 was made in the context of having recovered power narrowly in 1951 (a majority of 17 seats) on a smaller Liberal vote (48.0 per cent to Labour's 48.8 per cent, with the few Liberal candidates and the smaller Liberal vote being decisive). The Labour Party and the trade unions retained massive support and in 1952 in particular looked ready to return to office.

Churchill was determined not to derail his administration with major clashes with the trade unions. He appointed Sir Walter Monckton, a barrister whom Churchill had come to know when Monckton had advised Edward VIII during the abdication crisis, as Minister of Labour. Monckton, who declared, 'I am a firm believer in government by consultation and consent', secured industrial peace and was highly popular when he avoided a pre-Christmas rail strike in 1953. Churchill also sought successfully to avoid clashes with the miners, as coal exports were vital to British economic recovery. As Paul Addison has commented, 'A major strike leading to a run on the pound and savage deflationary measures might well have resulted in a Labour government.'[27]

After the great reforming Labour governments of 1945–51 Churchill also sought to show the Conservatives as being safe guardians of the Welfare State. Early proposals to make substantial welfare changes by the right-winger Harry Crookshank were much moderated and in under a year, in May 1952, Churchill replaced him as Minister of Health with Iain Macleod, a leading One Nation Group Conservative who was then 38. Churchill also wished to take action on the 1950 Conservative Party conference's call for 300,000 new houses to be built and encouraged Harold Macmillan, the Housing Minister, in his efforts to achieve large numbers of houses as well as substantial repairs to old housing stock.

In his speeches on domestic themes Churchill gave great emphasis to his government holding the moderate centre ground of British politics. Recognising the personal popularity of Attlee, Churchill often focused his attacks on Aneurin Bevan, the man he loved to loathe, and his left-wing supporters. At the 1953 Conservative Party conference he prefaced praise for Macmillan's housing achievements with reference to Bevan's 1948 Conservatives 'lower than vermin' speech, *One can quite understand how a politician who thinks more than half his fellow-countrymen are vermin cannot feel much enthusiasm for providing them with homes. 'Homes for vermin' can hardly seem an inspiring theme for the Socialist Party.* In contrast, he carefully praised trade unionists. At Glasgow in April 1953 he praised the trade union leaders for *their sense of responsibility* and their refusal *to allow the permanent interests of the wage earners to become the sport of party politics.* He went on, *I regard the trade unions as one of the outstanding institutions of our country … I have urged all Conservatives concerned to join them, to attend their meetings, and take a keen interest in their policy.*[28] In this he was back again to his understanding of Disraeli's 'Tory democracy'.

His domestic policy also involved the diminution of the role of the state and the boosting of private enterprise. In the 1951 general election his basic appeal had been 'of free enterprise and opportunity for all, and of the strong helping the weak', a romantic view of the decontrolled economy. However, his demands of an early ending of controls which affected the consumer had appealed to people tired of rationing and of very restricted choice. He came into office at the right time, as the 'golden age' of the international economy began, with substantial supplies of raw materials and manufactured goods and sustained levels of economic growth.

Given the serious doubts about his health from 1952, the most surprising aspect of Churchill's final term of office

Sir Winston Churchill received a state funeral at St Paul's Cathedral on 30 January 1965, the only commoner in the 20th century to be so honoured (the last had been the Duke of Wellington in 1852). He was to be buried at Bladon in Oxfordshire, next to his father, and after the service naval pallbearers carried his coffin to a barge on the Thames to be taken to Waterloo Station, the cranes along the river dipping in salute as it passed, and a flight of supersonic jets passing over the coffin of a man who had served in Queen Victoria's cavalry.

was that it was so long. Eden was angry and often moody about Churchill's repeated moving forward of the date of his departure. He even handed in his resignation in November 1953, but he failed to hurry him out. At one point Churchill even threatened his colleagues with the absurd idea that he might form a peace-seeking coalition government with the Labour Party. Eventually, the great romantic had to grasp that his time really had run out and he set 5 April 1955 as his resignation day. He ensured that he went out with style and dignity. He gave his wife a 70th birthday party at Downing Street on 1 April, with the Attlees present. Three days later the Churchills hosted a farewell dinner, with the Queen and the Duke of Edinburgh as the guests of honour. When he formally resigned, he declined the offer of a dukedom.

Churchill contested the general election held in May 1955. He enjoyed himself denouncing socialism and, in particular, Aneurin Bevan. The Liberals recommended that their supporters back Churchill 'who is still very much a Liberal'.[29] In 1959, in spite of him being 84 and Clementine's pleas for him not to stand again, Churchill contested the seat, making one public speech. His last years were often times of sadness. Like many elderly people, his friends found him happier talking of the past than the present. When he did speak of the present he reiterated favourite themes. For instance, shortly before his retirement, he was emphatic to Violet Bonham Carter, *We must* never *get out of step with the Americans – never*.[30] Yet he supported Eden's policies during the Suez crisis of 1956.

He did not contest the 1964 general election. He died, a national hero, on 24 January 1965, 70 years to the day after the death of his father.

Part Three

THE LEGACY

Chapter 7: Churchill's Premiership in Perspective

At the turn of this century Churchill was voted the greatest English person (with Isambard Kingdom Brunel second) in a BBC-organised poll of the British public. Some two decades earlier, before the ages of Thatcher and Blair, a room-full of historians specialising in twentieth century British history, when asked by A J P Taylor who they thought were three best British Prime Ministers of the 20th century to then, over-whelmingly came up with Churchill and Lloyd George, with Attlee and Macmillan (in that order) as leading contenders for third place.[1]

Churchill's high standing as a prime minister has nearly everything to do with the war years, not with the 1951–5 government. Nevertheless, Anthony Seldon has made a case for Churchill's leadership in 1951–3, but arguing that he should have gone by the autumn of 1954. Henry Pelling in his study of 1951–5, while recognising that 'Churchill was not able to assume in this administration the powerful position he had held during the war', believed that 'there was never any doubt that Churchill himself was the linchpin of his ministry, and his carefully prepared set-piece speeches provided the keynote of government policy'.[2] Churchill's position in 1951 rested on the popular admiration for his wartime achievements, the recognition by many in the Conservative Party that it would be highly impolitic to depose him and the fact that at the beginning of the government he still had something to offer in terms of status in international relations.

However, this was increasingly offset by his declining health. While Gladstone had declining hearing and eyesight, he was otherwise a fit man for his age when in his seventies and eighties (and forming three governments). Churchill gloried in his excesses: alcohol, cigars and food. R A Butler, for instance, wrote in his memoirs, that in Churchill's last four months, 'I had no less than eight gargantuan dinners with him alone; the dinners being followed by libations of brandy so ample that I felt it prudent on more than one occasion to tip the liquid into the side of my shoe.' Although under-performing, especially after his stroke in 1953, he suffered from the prime-ministerial malaise of being convinced that all others would do a far worse job. While ever seeking justification to go on for a little longer, he often reflected on the past. To Butler and others he commented on 'the difficulties of fag-end administrations (Rosebery after Gladstone, Balfour after Salisbury), both "brushed aside in spite of their ability, experience and charm" and a fairly clear indication that he would soldier on much closer to the election'.[3]

Churchill brought great experience to both his premierships. With his 1951–5 administration he at first built on his wartime system of co-ordinators, or overlords, for sectors of the government. He appointed Lords Cherwell, Woolton and Leathers, perhaps with the hope that their overseeing of large areas of domestic policy would free him up to concentrate not on waging war, as in 1940–5, but in seeking a secure peace. By 1953 he had to recognise that such a system did not work in peace conditions and he scrapped it. Generally, however, the fact that by the early 1950s he was a larger-than-life figure from an earlier political age and that he held an impressive past record of government experience that he usually ensured that he commanded respect in the Cabinet and in the House of Commons.

Churchill's post-war premiership set a pattern for the Conservatives' 13 years in office, 1951–64. Although Margaret Thatcher in office spoke of 'Winston' as if an old political friend and ally, he was, in her terminology, 'a wet', at least on domestic issues and quite probably in his seeking for peace through summit meetings at international level. Churchill saw his own political roots in his conception of Disraeli's and his father's 'Tory democracy'. He himself wanted to see a merger of Liberals with Conservatives, and he spoke on behalf of his friend Violet Bonham Carter in the Colne Valley in the 1951 general election, having got the local Conservatives not to oppose her and divide the anti-Socialist vote.

In 1940 Churchill already had massive experience when he came to the premiership. The national crisis put his particular qualities at a premium, and he was rightly seen as the Conservative politician most likely to display the fortitude and courage that Lloyd George had shown in 1916–18. He had generated great suspicion over the years, in particular arousing concern about his judgement. The writer Douglas Goldring, for instance, expressed some of the widespread doubts about Churchill in the early 1930s, when praising George Lansbury, the then Labour leader:

> What they said of Churchill:
>
> **Clement Attlee** said: 'Trouble with Winston. Nails his trousers to the mast. Can't get down.'
>
> **A J Balfour** said: 'I thought he was a young man of promise, but it appears he was a young man of promises.'
>
> **Aneurin Bevan** said: 'The mediocrity of his thinking is concealed by the majesty of his language.'
>
> **F E Smith** said: 'Winston has devoted the best years of his life to preparing his impromptu speeches.'

'Just as the brilliant Winston Churchill has every gift that a statesman should theoretically possess and only one defect, the fact that he is always wrong', so Lansbury, he argued was the opposite.[4] Churchill was not a man for all seasons, but a man to turn to in a highly inclement season. He had experienced war, he revelled in command over soldiers, sailors and police, and he was personally courageous and single minded. He also had some experience of wartime industrial organisation, having been Minister of Munitions, 1917–9 in the First World War, as well as government organisation.

What Churchill brought to wartime government was leadership. For all his reverence for the British constitution, he was determined to carry out the policies he felt essential for success and to put those he had confidence in into the key civilian and service roles. He and his Whitehall advisers built on the administrative lessons of the First World War. He surrounded himself with those he felt to be able advisers and, magpie-like, picked up their glittering ideas.[5] This could be very fruitful, or it could degenerate into cronyism. Beaverbrook was dynamic for short periods, but he was seen as a malign influence. Lesser figures, such as Brendan Bracken, were deemed to have been overpromoted. As for Liberals in his coalition, he preferred the gentlemanly Archie Sinclair and Harcourt Johnstone, both members of The Other Club, to other alternatives whom the Liberal Chief Whip would have recommended.[6]

Yet, while all governments arouse grumbles, generally his wartime government commanded respect. It had its 'downs', when the war was going badly. Yet it was, as Churchill claimed, a *most capable* coalition,[7] with figures such as Ernest Bevin and Clement Attlee for Labour playing impressive parts. Churchill, by dint of personality, hard work and oratory was the outstanding figure. He imprinted himself on the national consciousness not only by his stirring broadcasts but also by projecting very positive images (the hat, the cigar, the victory sign) and taking care to identify with those at the sharp end of the war effort (the fighter pilots, the Dunkirk evacuees, the homeless victims of enemy bombs and rockets, the merchant seamen).

While Prime Minister of a Coalition government, Churchill was alert to Conservative Party considerations. He was uneasy with some of Ernest Bevin's labour measures which boosted collective bargaining and reluctant to promise too much social reform when faced with the Beveridge Report. Amidst the pressing issues of war he made some efforts to protect Conservative and conservative interests for the resumption of party political conflict. Yet he often felt that the Conservative Party should be beholden to him. His Parliamentary Private Secretary noted his anger in January 1942, when the Conservatives in the House of Commons gave him a less than rapturous reception on his return from the United States, 'He said he alone had stood between the Tory Party and extinction'.[8] While this overstated matters, nevertheless as the war went on he knew that his party needed him, especially when it faced the electorate.

Churchill lived and breathed politics. His drive for success took its toll on his wife and his family. He saw his children more than Lord Randolph had, but his elder children nevertheless suffered from life with their overachieving father. Even his various relaxations were usually individualistic and achieving pastimes, such as painting or even bricklaying at Chartwell. He was remarkably self-centred, throughout life expecting people to jump to meet his requirements.

While Gladstone had admired Canning and Peel, Rosebery had been fascinated by Napoleon, Lloyd George acclaimed Abraham Lincoln, Churchill praised his ancestors and himself. By the time he reached the premiership he greatly enjoyed good food and alcohol and reminiscing. Joseph Lash, an American who sat next to him at a meal in late 1941, recalled, 'I was too awe-struck to open my mouth. There was no necessity. The language cascaded out of him.' Yet, like so many others, the older Churchill was fascinating, whether talking of Omdurman or of great politicians of the past. Joseph Lash wrote in his diary, 'He is an exuberant, enormously strong personality, exciting, full of temperament, witty, his phrases resonant with the vigors of the best English stylists, his talk full of imagery'.[9] Liking to hold forth at length was not just a feature of age. In 1956 Violet Bonham Carter was amused to hear of Churchill at Sandhurst from General Russell. 'He says he was bumptious, "held forth" – and was considered a bore by most people ... The General "rather liked him", in spite of the jaw, because of his intense keenness'. Winston Churchill then was already predicting that he would outshine his father.[10]

It was this keenness, openness and honesty that many of Churchill's oldest friends found most attractive. He had his depressions ('the black dog'), he could be brutal in his political actions but he could also be overwhelmingly generous. He mixed kindness with *noblesse oblige*. He genuinely cared for Mrs Everest and did his best for her last days. He similarly looked after those who served him well. His social policies were enlightened but can mostly be seen as paternalistic. The overwhelming impression of Churchill is of an able, ebullient aristocrat, playing the role in the nation's affairs that he felt to be his birthright.

While, like Lloyd George, his formative years had been in the Victorian period, his politics were flexible within democratic and free market boundaries. The dominant flavour of his politics was imperial, and this involved loyalty to the

Empire as it was in his travels of 1896–1908. He believed in the British Empire and its democratic-cultural role, as he saw it, in the world. He also saw it as the key to Britain remaining a superpower.

Ironically, he came to the premiership as the British Empire crumbled, and crumbled fast in the Far East. He believed in Great Men politics (with Great Women in politics being beyond his conception). He hoped to use his charisma to keep Britain at the international top table. He did achieve some rapport with Roosevelt and Truman, and to a lesser extent with Eisenhower and Stalin. But charisma and lengthy, albeit entertaining, monologues were not enough when Britain was a financial supplicant to the United States as was the case in the later years of the Second World War and also after it.

Churchill's beliefs in freedom and democracy were not confined to Britain and the British Empire. Half-American and throughout his adult life eager to earn dollars for lectures or publications, his world view encompassed the United States as well as the British Empire and Western Europe. He believed that his basic political and cultural aspirations could be forwarded by 'the English speaking peoples'. In this faith in the United States he was unusual among British politicians. Yet Churchill also admired France and other European countries. Churchill, although steeped in Empire, did look forward to the post-1945 world with United States hegemony and eventually a prosperous, democratic Europe.

NOTES

Chapter 1: Young Imperialist in a Hurry, 1874–1900

1. George Earle Buckle, *The Life of Benjamin Disraeli, Earl of Beaconsfield*, Vol 4 (John Murray, London: 1916) p 585.

2. George Earle Buckle, *The Life of Benjamin Disraeli, Earl of Beaconsfield*, Vol 5 (John Murray, London: 1920) p 312.

3. Winston S Churchill, *My Early Life* (Thornton, Butterworth, London: 1930) p 12, hereafter *My Early Life*.

4. Brian Tippett, 'An Isle of Wight Shipwreck: Hopkins, Churchill and the Loss of the Eurydice', *The Hatcher Review*, 5, 50 (2000) pp 41–50.

5. For the school reports, Randolph S Churchill, *Winston S. Churchill: Vol. 1, Youth* (Heinemann, London: 1966) pp 49–53, hereafter Churchill, *Youth*.

6. As well as being well-published on medical subjects, Dr Robson Roose (1848–1905) was a member of the Carlton and the Junior Carlton Clubs.

7. Celia Sandys, *From Winston With Love and Kisses: The Young Churchill* (Sinclair-Stevenson, London: 1994) p 66.

8. Letter of 16 March 1888, printed in Churchill, *Youth*, pp 108–9.

9. *My Early Life* (1959 paperback edn), p 25.

10. Churchill, *Youth*, pp 114–15, 119 and 123; *My Early Life*, p 29.

11. Churchill, *Youth*, p 116; Sandys, *From Winston With Love and Kisses*, pp 131–6.

12. Churchill, *Youth*, pp 181, 190–1 and 196.

13. Douglas S Russell, *Winston Churchill, Soldier. The Military Life of A Gentleman At War* (Brassey's, London: 2005) p 128. Churchill and Barnes were later awarded a second Cuba campaign medal by Spain.

14. Randolph S Churchill, *Winston S. Churchill*, Vol 1, *Companion* Part 1 (Heinemann, London: 1967) pp 617–18; Churchill, *My Early Life*, p 90.

15. Letter of 30 May 1909. Randolph S Churchill, *Winston S. Churchill*, Vol 2, *Companion* Part 2 (Heinemann, London: 1969) pp 893–4; James W Muller (ed), *Churchill's 'Iron Curtain' Speech Fifty Years Later* (University of Missouri, Columbia: 1999) p 6.

16. Churchill, *Youth,* p 281.

17. *My Early Life*, p 54; letter to Lady Randolph, 16 August 1895 in Churchill, *Youth*, p 259.

18. *My Early Life*, p 169.

19. Letter to Lady Randolph, 4 August 1896, Randolph S Churchill, *Winston S. Churchill*, Vol 1, *Companion* Part 1, pp 675–6.

20. His letters were published in the *Daily Telegraph*, 6 October–6 December 1897. Reprinted in Frederick Woods (ed), *Young Winston's Wars* (Seeley Service, London: 1972) pp 35–109.

21. John Keegan, *Churchill* (Weidenfeld and Nicolson, London: 2002) pp 37–40.

22. Letter to Lady Randolph, 9 December 1897, Randolph S Churchill, *Winston S. Churchill*, Vol 1, *Companion* Part 2, p 836.

23. *My Early Life*, p 159.

24. Winston S Churchill, *The River War* (third edn, Eyre and Spottiswoode, London: 1933) pp 360–2, 50, 7 and 34.

25. Russell, *Winston Churchill, Soldier*, pp 305–6 and 453.

Chapter 2: Imperialism, Social Reform and War, 1900–22

1. Robert Rhodes James, *Churchill: A Study in Failure 1900–1939* (Weidenfeld and Nicolson, London: 1970), references to Pelican edition, 1973. Roy Foster 'The Politics of Piety', his epilogue to *Lord Randolph Churchill. A Political Life* (Clarendon Press, Oxford: 1981) pp 383–403.

2. In *My Early Life*, pp 54–5.

3. WSC to Lady Randolph, 15 August 1902 and 14 September 1904, Randolph S Churchill, *Winston S. Churchill*, Vol 2, *Companion*, Part 1, pp 436 and 453. WSC to W St John Brodrick, 21 September 1904, Randolph S Churchill, *Winston S. Churchill*, Vol 2, *Companion*, Part 1, p 454.

4. His speech was reported extensively in the *Bath Daily Chronicle* and the *Morning Post*. Randolph S Churchill, *Winston S. Churchill*, Vol 1, *Companion*, Part 2, pp 770–4.

5. Violet Bonham Carter, *Winston Churchill As I Knew Him* (Eyre and Spottiswoode and Collins, London: 1965) pp 17–18.

6. WSC to Lady Randolph, 24 August 1897, Randolph S Churchill, *Churchill*, Vol 1, *Companion*, Part 2, p 779. Winston Spencer Churchill, *Savrola* (Longmans, Green, London: 1900. Quotations and references from Odhams' Beacon paperback edition, 1957) pp 80–1, 105, 209, 63 and 221. For examples of John Buchan's

and Sapper's subversive figures see *Huntingtower* (1922) and *The Black Gang* (1922).

7. Chris Wrigley, 'Churchill and the Trade Unions', *Transactions of the Royal Historical Society*, 6th series, 11 (2001) pp 273–93.

8. Winston S Churchill, *Mr Brodrick's Army* (Arthur Humphreys, London: 1903), a booklet dedicated to the electors of Oldham.

9. Winston S Churchill, 'Preface' to *For Free Trade* (Arthur Humphreys, London: 1906).

10. Ronald Hyam, *Elgin and Churchill at the Colonial Office, 1905–1908* (Macmillan, London: 1968) pp 12, 33 and 488–506.

11. Rhodes James, *Churchill: A Study in Failure*, p 38. Robert Rhodes James (ed), *Winston S. Churchill. His Complete Speeches*, Vol 1 (Chelsea House, London: 1974) pp 561–73 and 594–601, hereafter Rhodes James (ed), *Speeches*. Earl Winterton, 'Churchill the Parliamentarian', in Charles Eade (ed), *Churchill By His Contemporaries* (Hutchinson, London: 1953) pp.85–95. Randolph S Churchill, *Churchill*, Vol. 2, pp 182–3.

12. Margot Asquith, *More Memories* (Cassell, London: 1933) p 64.

13. Hyam, *Elgin And Churchill*, p 135.

14. Richard Jebb, *The Imperial Conference*, Vol 2 (Longmans Green, London: 1911) pp 241–5. Rhodes James (ed), *Speeches*, Vol 1, pp 782–3.

15. Churchill, *Youth*, p 296. Edward Marsh, *A Number Of People. A Book Of Reminiscences* (Heinemann, London: 1939) p 149.

16. G R Searle, *The Quest For National Efficiency* (Blackwell, Oxford: 1971) pp 248–50. Hyam, *Elgin And Churchill*, p 506.

17. Glasgow, 11 October 1906 and House of Commons, 28 April 1909, Rhodes James (ed), *Speeches*, Vol 1, pp 671–77 and Vol 2, pp 1221–7.

18. G R Searle, *Eugenics And Politics in Britain 1900–1914* (Noordhoff International, Leyden: 1976) pp 106–11.

19. Lucy Masterman, *C.F.G. Masterman. A Biography* (Cass, London: 1939) p 208.

20. Churchill, *Youth*, pp 523 and 526–8. Winston S Churchill, *The World Crisis*, Vol 1 (Thornton Butterworth, London: 1923; 1938 2-volume edition) Vol. 1, p 51.

21. Winston S Churchill, 'Preface' to Henry Longhurst, *Adventure In Oil. The Story of British Petroleum* (Sidgwick and Jackson, London: 1959).

22. Vice Admiral Sir Peter Gretton, *Former Naval Person. Winston Churchill and The Royal Navy* (Cassell, London: 1968).

23. Martin Gilbert, *Winston S. Churchill*, Vol. 3 (Heinemann, London: 1971). David Stafford, *Churchill And The Secret Service* (Murray, London: 1997).

24. Tuvia Ben-Moshe, *Churchill: Strategy and History* (Harvester-Wheatsheaf, Brighton: 1992). Robin Prior, *Churchill's 'World Crisis' As History* (Croom Helm, London: 1983).

25. Lord Riddell, *More Pages From My Diary* (Country Life, London: 1934).

26. Basil Thomson, *Queer People* (Hodder and Stoughton, London: n.d. [1922]) p 273. Trevor Wilson, *The Downfall of the Liberal Party* (Collins, London: 1966) p 137.

27. Martin Gilbert, *Winston S. Churchill*, Vol 4 (Heinemann, London: 1975) pp 251–4. Chris Wrigley, *Lloyd George*

and the Challenge of Labour (Harvester-Wheatsheaf, Brighton: 1990) pp 18–22.

28. Speech, 4 November 1920. Gilbert, *Churchill*, Vol 4, p 464.

29. *House of Commons Debates*, 8 July 1920. Gilbert, *Churchill*, Vol 4, pp 400–11

Chapter 3: In Defence of the British Empire and the Constitution, 1922–40

1. Paul Addison, *Churchill On The Home Front* (Cape, London: 1992) p 211.

2. Gilbert, *Churchill*, Vol 4, p 879.

3. Gilbert, *Churchill*, Vol 4, pp 13, 226 and 457.

4. Martin Gilbert, *Winston S. Churchill*, Vol 5 (Heinemann, London: 1976), p 16. Speech at Junior Training Hall, Leicester, 21 November 1923, Rhodes James (ed), *Speeches*, Vol 4, pp 3412–3.

5. *Daily Press* interview, 10 March 1924, and Adoption meeting, Exeter Hall, London, 10 March 1924, Rhodes James (ed), *Speeches*, Vol 4, pp 3435–8.

6. Speeches at Wanstead, 15 October, and Harlow, 16 October 1924, Rhodes James (ed), *Speeches*, Vol 4, pp 3489–91. The Epping seat was divided in 1945, Churchill becoming MP for the resulting Woodford seat, 1945–64. David A Thomas, *Churchill, The Member For Woodford* (Cass, London: 1995).

7. Michael Wolff, *Winston Churchill* (in the series 'The Great Nobel Prizes') (Edito Service/Heron Books, Geneva: 1970) p 160. Robin Prior, *Churchill's 'World Crisis' As History* (Croom Helm, London: 1983).

8. Speech at Manchester Free Trade Hall, 16 November 1923, Rhodes James (ed), *Speeches*, Vol 4, pp 3395–406.

Reginald McKenna had been Liberal Chancellor of the Exchequer, 1915–16.

9. Stuart Ball, 'Churchill and the Conservative Party', *Transactions of The Royal Historical Society*, 6th series, 11 (2001) pp 307–30.

10. Speech in the House of Commons, 3 May 1926, Rhodes James (ed), *Speeches*, Vol 4, pp 3946–53.

11. Robert Rhodes James (ed), *Memoirs of a Conservative* (Weidenfeld and Nicolson, London: 1969) p 243.

12. Speech at Sevenoaks, Kent, 27 April and election broadcast, 30 April 1929, Rhodes James (ed), *Speeches*, Vol 5, pp 4612–16.

13. Gilbert, *Winston S. Churchill*, Vol 5, pp 356 and 358–9.

14. Rhodes James (ed), *Speeches*, Vol 5, pp 4966–71.

15. Warren F Kimball (ed), *Churchill And Roosevelt. The Complete Correspondence*, Vol 1 (Princeton University Press, Princeton: 1984) p 24.

16. Mary Soames, *Winston Churchill. His Life AS A Painter* (Collins, London: 1990) p 74.

17. Martin Gilbert, *Churchill And America* (Free Press, London: 2005) pp 128–44. David Dilks, *'The Great Dominion'. Winston Churchill In Canada 1900–1954* (Thomas Allen, Toronto: 2005) pp 113–30.

18. Gilbert, *Churchill*, Vol 5, pp 406–9.

19. R A C Parker, *Churchill and Appeasement* (Macmillan, London: 2000), p 260.

Chapter 4: The British Empire Alone, 1940–1

1. Tom Hickman, *Churchill's Bodyguard* (Headline, London: 2005) p 71.

2. Sheila Lawlor, *Churchill And The Politics Of War, 1940–41* (Cambridge University Press, Cambridge: 1994); David Reynolds, *In Command Of History. Churchill*

Fighting and Writing the Second World War (Allen Lane, London: 2004).

3. Lord Hankey, *Government Control In War* (Cambridge University Press, Cambridge: 1945) pp 60–3. Speeches in House of Commons, 24 February and 2 July 1942, reprinted in Rhodes James (ed), *Speeches*, Vol 6, pp 6593–601 and 6656–7.

4. Lord Bridges in Sir John Wheeler-Bennett (ed), *Action This Day. Working With Churchill* (Macmillan, London: 1968) pp 218–40.

5. Sir Leslie Rowan in Wheeler-Bennett (ed), *Action This Day*, p 249. Hickman, *Churchill's Bodyguard*, p 59.

6. War Cabinet minutes, 13 June 1940. Cabinet Papers 65/7 and reprinted in Martin Gilbert (ed), *The Churchill War Papers*, Vol 2 (Heinemann, London: 1994) pp 319–22.

7. War Cabinet confidential annex, 16 June 1940. Cabinet Papers 65/13 and reprinted in Gilbert, *Churchill War Papers*, Vol 1, p 344.

8. Walter H Thompson, *Sixty Minutes With Winston Churchill* (Christopher Johnson, London: 1953) p 45; Lawlor, *Churchill and the Politics of War*, p 53.

9. Earl of Woolton, *Memoirs Of The Earl of Woolton* (Cassell, London: 1959) p 280.

10. Rhodes James (ed), *Speeches*, Vol 6, p 6231.

11. Thompson, *Sixty Minutes With Winston Churchill*, p 53. Hickman, *Churchill's Bodyguard*, pp 106 and 108.

12. David Stafford, *Roosevelt and Churchill. Men of Secrets* (Little and Brown, London, 1999; paperback, Abacus, London: 2000) pp 38–44.

13. G S Harvie-Watt, *Most Of My Life* (Springwood Books, London: 1980) p 130. Andrew Roberts, *Hitler And*

Churchill. Secrets of Leadership (Weidenfeld and Nicolson, London: 2003; Phoenix paperback: 2004) p 135.

14. Churchill to Robert Menzies and William MacKenzie King, 12 December, and to President Roosevelt, 13 December 1940, Gilbert (ed), *Churchill War Papers*, Vol 2, pp 1222 and 1225–6.

15. Quoted in Lawlor, *Churchill and the Politics of War*, p 192.

16. A J P Taylor, *The Second World War* (Hamish Hamilton, London: 1975) p 91.

17. Martin Gilbert (ed), *The Churchill War Papers*, Vol 3 (Heinemann, London: 2000) p 702.

18. John Colville, *The Fringes of Power. Downing Street Diaries 1939–1955* (Hodder and Stoughton, London: 1985) p 391. Gilbert (ed), *Churchill War Papers*, Vol 3, p 715.

19. Rhodes James, *Speeches*, Vol 6, pp 6427–31.

20. Churchill minute to First Sea Lord, the Secretary of State for War, the Secretary of State for Air and the Minister of Shipping, 30 April 1941, Gilbert (ed), *Churchill War Papers*, Vol 3, pp 578–9; Taylor, *Second World War*, p 80.

21. Rhodes James, *Speeches*, Vol 6, pp 6502–5; Gilbert (ed), *Churchill War Papers*, Vol 3, pp 1574 and 1580.

Chapter 5: Grand Alliance but Gradual Decline, 1941–5

1. Lord Bridges in Wheeler-Bennett, *Action This Day*, p 236.

2. John Charmley, *Churchill's Grand Alliance* (Hodder and Stoughton, London: 1995) p xiv.

3. Captain Cunningham-Reid, *Besides Churchill – Who?* (W H Allen, London: 1942) pp 93–4. He was a

Conservative MP 1922–3, 1924–9, 1932–42 and Independent MP, 1942–5.

4. Diary entries, 11 August 1940 and 20–21 January 1945, Colville, *Fringes Of Power*, pp 220 and 544–5.

5. Walter H Thompson, *I Was Churchill's Shadow* (Johnston, London: 1951).

6. Coln Thornton-Kemsley, *Through Winds And Tides* (Standard Press, Montrose: 1974) p 35.

7. Field Marshal Lord Alanbrooke, *War Diaries 1939–1945* (ed A Danchev and D Todman) (Weidenfeld and Nicolson, London: 2001) pp 459, 524–5 and 532.

8. Rhodes James (ed), *Speeches*, Vol 6, pp 6480–2.

9. Rhodes James (ed), *Speeches*, Vol 6, pp 6693–5.

10. Reynolds, *In Command Of History*, p 264.

11. Martin Gilbert, *Winston S. Churchill*, Vol 7 (Heinemann, London: 1986) pp 300–2. Richard Wigg, *Churchill And Spain. The Survival of the Franco Regime, 1940–45* (Routledge, London: 2005), especially pp 190–1. Rhodes James (ed), *Speeches*, Vol 6, p 6694.

12. Roberts, *Hitler And Churchill*, pp 128–9.

13. Diary 14 September 1944, Colville, *Fringes Of Power*, p 514.

14. Edward R Stettinius memorandum, 13 April 1943. Gilbert, *Churchill*, Vol 7, p 1295.

15. Martin Gilbert, *Churchill: A Life* (Heinemann, London: 1991) pp 783–4.

16. Rhodes James (ed), *Speeches*, Vol 7, pp 7152–3, 7155 and 7169–74.

17. Gilbert, *Churchill: A Life*, p 847.

18. Paul Addison, *The Road To 1945* (Cape, London: 1975) p 276.

Chapter 6: Cold War and The End of Empire, 1945–65

1. Mary Soames, *Clementine Churchill* (Cassell, London: 1979) pp 386–7 and 390–3.
2. Reynolds, *In Command Of History*, p xxv.
3. Diary, 13 February 1945, Colville, *The Fringes Of Power*, p 559.
4. In this instance a speech of 14 October 1947, Rhodes James (ed), *Speeches*, Vol 7, p 7540.
5. Winston S Churchill, *A History Of The English-Speaking Peoples*, Vol 1 (Cassell, London: 1956) pp vii–viii.
6. Rhodes James (ed), *Speeches*, Vol 7, pp 7379–82.
7. Rhodes James (ed), *Speeches*, Vol 7, pp 7285–93.
8. John Ramsden, 'Mr Churchill Goes to Fulton', in James W Muller (ed), *Churchill's 'Iron Curtain' Speech Fifty Years Later* (University of Missouri Press, Columbia: 1999) pp 15–47.
9. John Young, *Winston Churchill's Last Campaign. Britain and the Cold War, 1951–1955* (Clarendon Press, Oxford: 1996) pp 25–8.
10. Rhodes James (ed), *Speeches*, Vol 8, p 7944.
11. On 4 October 1947, Rhodes James (ed), *Speeches*, Vol 7, p 7532.
12. Rhodes James (ed), *Speeches*, Vol 8, pp 7927, 7941, 7944–6 and 8260.
13. Young, *Winston Churchill's Last Campaign*, p 310.
14. Soames, *Clementine Churchill*, p 436.
15. Mark Pottle (ed), *Daring To Hope. The Diaries and Letters of Violet Bonham Carter 1946–1969* (Weidenfeld and Nicolson, London: 2000) p 230.
16. Anthony Seldon, *Churchill's Indian Summer. The Conservative Government 1951–55* (Hodder and Stoughton, London: 1981) pp 411 and 622; William Roger Louis, 'Churchill and Egypt' in Robert Blake

and William Roger Louis (eds), *Churchill* (Oxford University Press, Oxford: 1993) pp 473–90.

17. Sir Anthony Eden, *Full Circle* (Cassell, London: 1960) pp 245–7.

18. Seldon, *Churchill's Indian Summer*, pp 389–91. Peter Boyle, 'The "Special Relationship" with Washington', in John W Young (ed), *The Foreign Policy Of Churchill's Peacetime Administration, 1951–1955* (Leicester University Press, Leicester: 1988) pp 29–54.

19. Young, *Winston Churchill's Last Campaign*, pp 77–82.

20. David Carlton, *Churchill and The Soviet Union* (Manchester University Press, Manchester: 2000) p 177.

21. Peter G Boyle (ed), *The Churchill-Eisenhower Correspondence 1953–1955* (University of North Carolina Press, Chapel Hill: 1990) p 31.

22. Rhodes James (ed), *Speeches*, Vol 8, p 8470.

23. Rhodes James (ed), *Speeches*, Vol 8, pp 8483–5.

24. Rhodes James (ed), *Speeches*, Vol 8, pp 8496–7. Klaus Larres, *Churchill's Cold War. The Politics Of Personal Diplomacy* (Yale University Press, New Haven and London: 2002) pp 360–1.

25. Young, *Winston Churchill's Last Campaign*, p 223.

26. Martin Gilbert, *Winston S Churchill*, Vol 8 (Heinemann, London: 1988) p 1025.

27. Paul Addison, *Churchill On The Home Front* (Cape, London: 1992) pp 412–4.

28. Rhodes James (ed), *Speeches*, Vol 8, pp 8491 and 8466.

29. David A Thomas, *Churchill. The Member for Woodford* (Cass, London: 1995) pp 176–7.

30. Pottle (ed), *Daring To Hope*, pp 147 and 224.

Chapter 7: Churchill's Premiership in Perspective

1. For an admirable study of the development of Churchill's reputation since 1945, see John Ramsden, *Man Of The Century* (Harper Collins, London: 2002).

2. Seldon, *Churchill's Indian Summer*, especially Chapters 2 and 3 and epilogue 3. Henry Pelling, *Churchill's Peacetime Ministry 1951–55* (Macmillan, London: 1997) pp 178 and 183.

3. Lord Butler, *The Art Of The Possible* (Hamish Hamilton, London: 1971) pp 174 and 176.

4. Douglas Goldring, *Odd Man Out* (Chapman and Hall, London: 1935) p 268.

5. Kevin Theakston, *Winston Churchill and the British Constitution* (Politicos, London: 2004) p 232.

6. Addison, *The Road To 1945*, p 105. Gerald de Groot, *Liberal Crusader. The Life of Sir Archibald Sinclair* (Hurst, London: 1993).

7. J M Lee, *The Churchill Coalition 1940–1945* (Batsford, London: 1980) p 176.

8. G S Harvie-Watt, *Most Of My Life* (Springwood Books, London: 1980) p 74.

9. Joseph P Lash, *Roosevelt And Churchill 1939–1941. The Partnership that saved the West* (Andre Deutsch, London: 1977) p 15.

10. Pottle (ed), *Daring To Hope*, p 171.

CHRONOLOGY

Year	Premiership

1940
10 May: Winston Churchill becomes Prime Minister, aged 65.
BEF evacuated from Dunkirk.
Churchill makes 'fight on the beaches' speech.
Churchill orders destruction of Vichy French fleet at Oran.
The Battle of Britain.
Failed Free French and British attack on Dakar.
Churchill becomes Conservative leader after Chamberlain resigns due to ill health.
Italian fleet crippled by British carrier aircraft at Taranto.
Wavell defeats the Italians in Libya.

1941
British troops sent to Greece – withdrawn in April.
Fall of Crete. Rommel commands German/Italian forces in Libya, attacks Tobruk.
German battleship *Bismarck* sinks the *Hood*: *Bismarck* sunk two days later.
Churchill announces British support for USSR after German invasion.
Tobruk is relieved by British who advance across Libya.
Churchill meets Roosevelt aboard *Prince of Wales* in Placentia Bay.
Britain declares war on Japan after Pearl Harbor.
HMS *Prince of Wales* and *Repulse* sunk by Japanese aircraft.

1942
Rommel launches counter-offensive against British.
Surrender of Singapore to Japanese.
Japanese invade Burma.
Rommel retakes Tobruk in Libya, British retreat.
Montgomery defeats Rommel at El Alamein.
Beveridge Report on Social Insurance and Allied Services published.

1943
Churchill meets Roosevelt at Casablanca: agree unconditional surrender for Germany and Japan.
Beveridge Report accepted by Parliament.
Rommel retreats in North Africa; US and British link up; Germans in Tunisia surrender.
Invasion of Sicily.
Churchill meets Roosevelt at Quebec Conference.
Tehran Conference: Roosevelt, Stalin and Churchill meet.

History	Culture
Second World War.	Kandinsky, *Sky Blue.*
Germany invades Holland, Belgium, Luxembourg.	Graham Greene, *The Power and the Glory.*
Italy declares war on France and Britain.	Ernest Hemingway, *For Whom the Bell Tolls.*
France divides into German-occupied north and Vichy south.	Eugene O'Neill, *Long Days Journey into Night.*
Roosevelt is elected for an unprecedented third term as US president.	Films: *The Great Dictator. Pinocchio. Rebecca.*
Hungary and Romania join Axis.	
Italy invades Greece.	
Second World War.	Etienne Gilson, *God and Philosophy.*
Germany invades USSR	
Japanese troops occupy Indochina.	Bertold Brecht, *Mother Courage and Her Children.*
Germans besiege Leningrad and Moscow.	Noel Coward, *Blithe Spirit.*
Soviets counter-attack at Moscow.	British communist paper, *The Daily Worker*, is suppressed.
Japan attacks Pearl Harbor,	
Japan invades Philippines.	Films: *Citizen Kane. Dumbo. The Maltese Falcon.*
Germany and Italy declare war on the USA.	
Atomic bomb development begins in USA.	
Second World War.	Shostakovich, *Symphony No. 7.*
Wannsee Conference for Final Solution held in Germany.	Frank Sinatra's first stage performance in New York.
US surrender in Philippines.	Albert Camus, *The Outsider.*
Dolittle Raid: US bombs Tokyo.	T S Eliot, *Little Gidding.*
US invasion of Guadalcanal turns Japanese tide.	Jean Anouilh, *Antigone.*
	Films: *Casablanca. How Green was my Valley.*
Battle of Stalingrad in USSR. Eisenhower lands in Morocco and Algeria.	
Second World War.	Hoffman discovers LSD.
German withdrawal from Russia begins.	Jean-Paul Sartre, *Being and Nothingness.*
Beleaguered Romanians and Germans surrender to Russians at Stalingrad.	Henry Moore, *Madonna and Child.*
Italian King dismisses Mussolini and asks Badoglio to form a government.	Rogers and Hammerstein, *Oklahoma!*
Italy surrenders unconditionally. New Italian government declares war on Germany.	Jean-Paul Sartre, *The Flies.*
	Film: *For Whom the Bell Tolls. Bataan.*

Year	Premiership

1944 6 June: D-Day landings in France. Churchill visits Montgomery's HQ soon after invasion.
Churchill attends second Quebec Conference.
Churchill visits Moscow for talks with Stalin.
British 'Butler' Education Act divides education into primary, secondary and further stages, introduces 11+ exams.

1945 Yalta Conference: last meeting of the 'Big Three'.
RAF bombing of Dresden.
8 May: VE Day – Churchill feted by crowds in London.
26 July: Churchill loses election in landslide win for Labour Party lead by Clement Attlee

1951 26 October: Churchill returns to Downing Street as both Prime Minister and Minister of Defence, as during the War.
Leaves to visit USA and Canada

1952 Churchill meets President Truman in Washington.
King George VI dies: Elizabeth II becomes Queen.
Field Marshal Alexander takes over as Minister of Defence.
State of emergency proclaimed in Kenya due to Mau Mau uprising.

History	Culture
British and US forces in Italy liberate Rome.	Carl Jung, *Psychology and Religion*.
Claus von Stauffenberg's bomb at Rastenburg fails to kill Hitler.	Michael Tippett, *A Child of Our Time*.
British and US forces in Italy liberate Rome.	T S Eliot, *Four Quartets*.
Free French enter Paris.	Terrence Rattigan, *The Winslow Boy*.
Roosevelt wins fourth term in office.	Tennessee Williams, *The Glass Menagerie*.
German counter-offensive in the Ardennes.	Film: *Double Indemnity*. *Henry V*. *Meet Me in St Louis*.
	Radio: *Much-Binding-in-the-Marsh*.
Second World War.	Karl Popper, *The Open Society and its Enemies*.
British troops invade Burma.	Benjamin Britten, *Peter Grimes*.
Roosevelt dies and is succeeded by Truman.	Arts Council of Great Britain is established.
Soviet Army takes Vienna and advances to Berlin.	George Orwell, *Animal Farm*.
Mussolini is shot and his body is displayed in Milan.	Jean-Paul Sartre, *The Age of Reason*.
Germans surrender on Italian front.	Evelyn Waugh, *Brideshead Revisited*.
Hitler commits suicide in Berlin, and the city surrenders to Soviets.	Films: *Brief Encounter*. *The Way to the Stars*.
Peron is re-elected president of Argentina.	Benjamin Britten, *Billy Budd*.
Electric power is produced from atomic energy in USA.	Isaac Asimov, *Foundation*.
	J D Salinger, *The Catcher in the Rye*.
	Herman Wouk, *The Caine Mutiny*.
	Film: *A Streetcar Named Desire*. *The African Queen*.
Arab League Security Pact comes into force.	Henry Moore, *King and Queen*.
Iran breaks diplomatic relations with Britain over oil dispute.	John Cage, *4'33"*.
King Farouk of Egypt deposed.	Michael Tippett, *The Midsummer Marriage*.
Eisenhower wins US Presidential election in a landslide victory.	Dylan Thomas, *Collected Poems*.
Contraceptive pill produced in the USA.	Evelyn Waugh, *Men at Arms*.
USA explodes first hydrogen bomb in Pacific.	Agatha Christie, *The Mousetrap*.
	Films: *Singin' in the Rain*. *High Noon*. *Limelight*. *The Quiet Man*.
	Radio: *The Goon Show*.

Year	Premiership
1953	Churchill visits new US President Eisenhower in Washington.
	Sugar rationing ends in Britain.
	Churchill receives Yugoslav leader Tito in London.
	Churchill takes over as Foreign Secretary while Eden ill.
	Churchill calls for summit meeting with the USSR after Stalin's death.
	Coronation of Queen Elizabeth II.
	Churchill suffers serious stroke.
	Churchill's speech at Conservative Conference in October marks recovery from stroke.
	Churchill attends delayed Bermuda Conference.
	Rail strike avoided.
1954	Churchill reveals details of wartime Quebec agreement in Commons debate.
	Cabinet resignations threatened over Churchill's offer of summit to Soviets without consulting Cabinet.
	Anglo-Egyptian Agreement for British withdrawal from Canal Zone signed.
	Rationing ends.
	Government sets up Wolfenden Committee to enquire into homosexuality and prositution.
1955	5 April: Churchill resigns, having served all together 8 years and 240 days as premier.

History	Culture
Yugoslav National Assembly adopts new constitution. Tito is elected first president of Yugoslav Republic. European Political Community constitution is drafted and later adopted. Josef Stalin dies. In USSR, Nikita Khrushchev is appointed first secretary of central committee of Communist Party. Konrad Adenauer forms new government in West Germany.	Ludwig Wittgenstein, *Philosophical Investigations*. Benjamin Britten, *Gloriana*. Shostakovich, *Symphony No. 10*. Arthur Miller, *The Crucible*. BBC television broadcast of the Coronation is first major TV event. Films: *The Big Heat. From Here to Eternity. Gentlemen Prefer Blondes. Julius Caesar*.
In USA, Eisenhower makes broadcast about H-bomb and the communist threat. Armistice for Indochina is signed; France evacuates N Vietnam, Ho Chi Minh forms government. South-East Asian Defence treaty and Pacific Charter signed; SEATO established.	Britten, *The Turn of the Screw*. Kingsley Amis, *Lucky Jim*. William Golding, *Lord of the Flies*. J R R Tolkein, *The Lord of the Rings I, II. (III in 1955)* Tennessee Williams, *Cat on a Hot Tin Roof*. Films: *On the Waterfront. Rear Window. The Seven Samurai*. Radio: *Hancock's Half Hour*.

FURTHER READING

With many books on Churchill being published each year, this list provides only an introduction to a few of the more recent and more important books. The major resources on Churchill are the official biography, *Winston S. Churchill* (published in London by Heinemann), the first two volumes by Randolph Churchill (1966–7) and the final six volumes by Sir Martin Gilbert (1971–88), with 16 huge companion volumes of documents so far (1967–2000), and the eight large volumes, *Churchill Speaks: Collected Speeches, 1897–1963* (Chelsea House and Bowker, New York: 1981), edited by Robert Rhodes James. For Churchill's books see Frederick Woods, *A Bibliography of the Works of Sir Winston Churchill* (Nicholas Vane, London: 1963) or for a sizeable general bibliography see the end of Chris Wrigley, *Churchill: A Biographical Companion* (ABC-Clio, Santa Barbara, California: 2002).

Addison, Paul, *Churchill* (Oxford University Press, Oxford: 2005).

—, *Churchill On The Home Front* (Cape, London: 1992).

Ben-Moshe, Tuvia, *Churchill: Strategy And History* (Harvester-Wheatsheaf, Hemel Hempstead: 1992).

Blake, Robert and W R Louis (eds), *Churchill* (Oxford University Press, Oxford: 1993).

Cannadine, David and R Quinault (eds), *Churchill in the Twenty-First Century* (Cambridge University Press, Cambridge: 2004).

Carlton, David, *Churchill and the Soviet Union* (Manchester University Press, Manchester: 2000).

Charmley, John, *Churchill: The End Of Glory* (Hodder and Stoughton, London: 1993).

Hyam, Ronald, *Elgin and Churchill at the Colonial Office* (Macmillan, London: 1968).

Jenkins, Roy, *Churchill* (Macmillan, London: 2001).

Lawlor, Sheila, *Churchill And The Politics Of War, 1940–1941* (Cambridge University Press, Cambridge: 1994).

Parker, R A C, *Churchill And Appeasement* (Macmillan, London: 2000).

— (ed), *Winston Churchill: Studies In Statesmanship* (Brasseys, London: 1995).

Prior, Robin, *Churchill's 'World Crisis' As History* (Croom Helm, London: 1983).

Ramsden, John, *Man of The Century: Winston Churchill And His Legend Since 1945* (Harper Collins, London: 2002).

Roskill, Stephen, *Churchill and the Admirals* (Collins, London: 1977).

Reynolds, David, *In Command Of History. Churchill Fighting and Writing the Second World War* (Allen Lane, London: 2004).

Russell, Douglas S, *Winston Churchill: Soldier* (Brasseys, London: 2005).

Seldon, Anthony, *Churchill's Indian Summer 1951–55* (Hodder and Stoughton, London: 1981).

Soames, Mary, *Clementine Churchill* (Cassell, London: 1979).

Stafford, David, *Churchill and the Secret Service* (Murray, London: 1997).

Wheeler-Bennett, Sir John (ed), *Action This Day. Working with Churchill* (Macmillan, London: 1968).

Young, John, *Winston Churchill's Last Campaign* (Oxford University Press, Oxford: 1996).

PICTURE SOURCES

Pages vi–vii
Churchill gives his famous V for victory sign to a crowd of
more than 50,000 from a balcony at the Ministry of Health
on 8 May 1945. He stands between Clement Attlee (on
his left) and Ernest Bevin (on his right). (Courtesy Topham
Picturepoint)

Page 100
Churchill inspects north-eastern coastal defences in 1940.
(Courtesy Topham Picturepoint)

Pages 130–1
Churchill and Charles de Gaulle inspect a guard of
honour during a visit to Paris in 1951. (Courtesy Topham
Picturepoint)

INDEX

A

Acheson, Dean 110
Alexander, A V 74
Anderson, John 70
Anderson, Torr 65
Amery, Leo 66
Asquith, H H 29, 30, 31, 34, 36, 38, 42, 43, 44, 51, 60, 78
Asquith, Margot 31
Attlee, Clement 88, 89, 101, 106, 110, 112, 116, 118, 120, 125, 126
Auchinleck, Claude 74, 80, 83

B

Babington Macaulay, Thomas 7
Baldwin, Stanley 54, 56, 57, 60, 62, 64, 65
Balfour, Arthur 5, 28, 29, 47, 51, 124
Barnes, Reginald 11, 12
Barrymore, Ethel 34
Battenberg, Louis 40, 42
Bracken, Brendan 65, 88, 126

Beatty, David 18
Beaverbrook, Lord 62, 71, 73, 74, 88, 108, 126
Beresford, William 14
Beveridge, William 99, 127
Bevan, Aneurin ('Nye') 108, 118, 125
Bevin, Ernest 88, 98, 106, 112, 126, 127
Blair, Tony 101, 123
Blood, Bindon 14, 15, 16
Bonar Law, Andrew 43, 44
Bonham Carter, Violet 25, 109, 120, 125, 128
Boothby, Robert 65
Bourke Cochran, William 12
Botha, Louis 19
Brabazon, John 9, 10, 11
Bridges, Edward 72, 85, 89
Brodrick, John 27, 28
Brook, Alan 90, 91, 95
Buller, Redvers 19
Burke, Edmund 16
Butler, Richard Austen ('Rab') 107, 108, 124

C

Cadogan, Alexander 82, 91

Campbell-Bannerman, Henry 29, 30

Cartland, Ronald 66

Chamberlain, Austen 13, 51

Chamberlain, Joseph 28, 29, 85

Chamberlain, Neville 60, 64, 66, 67, 70, 72, 78, 79, 87

Cherwell, Lord 124

Churchill, Clementine 53, 54, 88, 101, 102, 115, 120

Churchill, Diana (oldest daughter) 34

Churchill, Gwendeline ('Goonie', sister-in-law) 63

Churchill, John Strange ('Jack', brother) 3, 5, 6

Churchill, John Winston, 7th Duke of Marlborough (grand-father) 1

Churchill, Marigold (third daughter, who died aged two) 34

Churchill, Mary (youngest daughter, later Mary Soames) 34, 63, 76, 109

Churchill, Lady Randolph (mother, also see Jennie Jerome) 4, 6, 10, 14, 15, 33

Churchill, Lord Randolph (father) 1, 2, 4, 6, 8, 9, 10, 11, 12, 21, 22, 23, 24, 28, 29, 57, 120

Churchill, Randolph (son) 34, 90

Churchill, Sarah (second daughter) 34, 99

Colville, John 88

Cooper, Duff 66

Cranborne, Lord (later Salisbury) 66

Cripps, Stafford 88, 89, 98

Crookshank, Harry 118

D

Davidson, J C C 59

de Gaulle, Charles 74, 78, 87

Denikin, Anton 47

Dilke, Charles 85

Disraeli, Benjamin 1, 2, 15, 16, 24, 28, 69, 102, 107

Donovan, William 76

Douglas-Home, Alec 101

Dyer, Reginald 48, 50

E

Eden, Anthony 66, 70, 80,

97, 101, 102, 109, 110, 112, 113, 116, 119, 120
Edward VII, King 39
Edward VIII, King 65, 117
Eisenhower, Dwight 103, 110, 113, 116, 129
Elgin, Lord 16, 30, 31
Elizabeth I, Queen 75
Elizabeth II, Queen 108, 120
Everest, Elizabeth Ann 3, 4, 5, 6, 26, 128

F
Fisher, John ('Jackie') 39, 42
Franco, Francisco 70, 94

G
Gandhi, Mohandas Karamchand ('Mahatma') 61
George VI, King 98
Gibbon, Edward 13, 16, 18
Gladstone, Herbert 13
Gladstone, William Ewart 4, 21, 69, 76, 101, 109, 114, 124, 127
Gordon, Lord 18
Gretton, Peter 40

H
Haig, Douglas 18, 42

Haile Selassie (Abyssinian Emperor) 82
Haldane, R B 38
Halifax, Lord 70, 87
Harris, Arthur 97
Harvie-Watt, G S 79
Hastings, Warren 31
Healey, Denis 69
Henlein, Conrad 66
Hitler, Adolf 53, 63, 64, 67, 73, 82, 89
Hogg, Douglas (later Lord Hailsham) 60
Hozier, Clementine (wife, also see Clementine Churchill) 34

I
Irwin, Lord (ater Viscount Halifax) 61

J
James, W H 8, 9
Jellicoe, John 40
Jerome, Jennie (mother, also see Lady Randolph Churchill) 1, 2
Jerome, Leonard (grand-father) 2
Johstone, Harcourt 126

K
Kautsky, Karl 26

Kent, Tyler 76
Keynes, John Maynard 58
Kitchener, Lord 17, 20, 40, 42, 56

L

Lansbury, George 125, 126
Lavery, Hazel 63
Lavery, John 63
Leathers, Lord 124
Lecky, William 13
Leeper, Reginald 65
Lindemann, Frederick 64, 66, 103
Lloyd George, David 5, 25, 29, 31, 32, 33, 34, 35, 36, 37, 38, 42, 43, 44, 45, 46, 49, 50, 51, 56, 57, 60, 70, 72, 78, 91, 101, 108, 123, 125, 129
Lockhart, William 17

M

Macaulay, Lord 31, 62
MacDonald, Ramsay 61, 101
Macmillan, Harold 66, 101, 118
Mahdi, (Mohammed Ahmed) 18, 19
Marlborough, Duke of 23, 52, 62, 63, 71
Marsh, Edward 32

Masterman, Charles 35
Masterman, Lucy 37
Mawdsley, James 27
McKenna, Reginald 38, 57, 58
Milner, Alfred 45, 85
Molotov, V M (Skriabin) 116
Monckton, Walter 64, 117
Monnet, Jean 74
Montgomery, Bernard Law 73, 80, 89, 95, 115
Morgenthau, Henry 95
Morel, E G 50
Morley, John 24
Morrison, Herbert 98
Morton, Desmond 65
Mussolini, Benito 52, 53, 70, 80, 94

N

Napoleon (French Emperor) 82, 127
Nicolson, Harold 62

P

Parnell, Charles Stewart 31
Peel, Robert 51, 127
Pétain, Marshal 74
Pick, Frank 74
Plowden, Pamela 33
Pound, Dudley 74

R

Reith, John 61
Riddell, Lord 46
Roberts, Lord 17, 20
Robertson, William 91
Rommel, Erwin 80
Roose, Robson 6
Roosevelt, Franklin Delano
    63, 76, 78, 80, 86, 91,
    92, 94, 95, 96, 101,
    129
Rosebery, Lord 35, 85, 124,
    127
Rothschild, Lionel 34
Rowan, Leslie 73
Russell, General 128

S

Salisbury, (Robert Cecil, 3rd
    Marquis of Salisbury) 5,
    17, 28, 124
Salisbury, Lord (formerly
    Lord Cranborne) 108,
    115
Sandys, Duncan (son-in-
    law) 66
Scrivings, George 32, 33
Scrymgeour, Edwin 50, 52
Sickert, Walter 63
Sinclair, Archie 126
Simpson, Wallis 64, 65
Smith, F E 32, 50, 51, 70,
    89, 125

Smuts, Jan Christiaan 95
Somervell, Robert 7
Spee, Maximilian 41
Stalin, Joseph 89, 93, 95,
    96, 102, 105, 106, 113,
    129
Stephenson, William 76
Stevenson, Robert Louis 7

T

Thatcher, Margaret 101,
    123, 125
Thomas, J P L 66
Thompson, Walter H 48,
    69, 90
Thomson, Basil 45
Thomson, Charlotte 6
Thomson, Kate 6
Thornton-Kemsley, Colin
    90
Tito, Josip 95, 103
Tree, Ronald 66
Trenchard, Hugh 49
Truman, Harry S 96, 101,
    106, 110, 112, 113,
    129
Tweedmouth, 34

V

Vane-Tempest, Henry 56
Vansittart, Robert 65
Victoria, Queen 17, 85
Vincent, Helen 34

W

Wavell, Field Marshal 79, 80, 81

Webb, Beatrice 25

Webb, Sidney 35

Weitzman, Chaim 97

Welldon, J E C 7, 8

Wigram, Ralph 65

William II, Kaiser (German Emperor) 38

Wilson, Gordon 32

Wilson, Henry 91

Wilson, Muriel 34

Wood, Kingsley 79

Woolton, Lord 124

Wolseley, Lord 11, 17

THE 20 BRITISH PRIME MINISTERS
OF THE 20TH CENTURY

SALISBURY by Eric Midwinter	ISBN 1-904950-54-X
BALFOUR by Ewen Green	ISBN 1-904950-55-8
CAMPBELL-BANNERMAN by Lord Hattersley	ISBN 1-904950-56-6
ASQUITH by Stephen Bates	ISBN 1-904950-57-4
LLOYD GEORGE by Hugh Purcell	ISBN 1-904950-58-2
BONAR LAW by Andrew Taylor	ISBN 1-904950-59-0
BALDWIN by Anne Perkins	ISBN 1-904950-60-4
MACDONALD by Kevin Morgan	ISBN 1-904950-61-2
CHAMBERLAIN by Graham Macklin	ISBN 1-904950-62-0
CHURCHILL by Chris Wrigley	ISBN 1-904950-63-9
ATTLEE by David Howell	ISBN 1-904950-64-7
EDEN by Peter Wilby	ISBN 1-904950-65-5
MACMILLAN by Francis Beckett	ISBN 1-904950-66-3
DOUGLAS-HOME by David Dutton	ISBN 1-904950-67-1
WILSON by Paul Routledge	ISBN 1-904950-68-X
HEATH by Denis MacShane MP	ISBN 1-904950-69-8
CALLAGHAN by Harry Conroy	ISBN 1-904950-70-1
THATCHER by Clare Beckett	ISBN 1-904950-71-X
MAJOR by Robert Taylor	ISBN 1-904950-72-8
BLAIR by Mick Temple	ISBN 1-904950-73-6

Boxed Set
(all 20 books plus
TIMELINE OF THE
20TH CENTURY
extra and only available
as part of the boxed set):
ISBN 1-904950-53-1